D0614166

Innovative Turkey Hunting

ADVANCED TACTICS FROM
BRAD HARRIS & MARK DRURY

799.248645 C261
Casada, Jim.
Innovative turkey hunting
                    19.95

MID-CONTINENT PUBLIC LIBRARY
Blue Ridge Branch
9253 Blue Ridge Boulevard
Kansas City, Mo. 64138

BR

Jim Casada

WITHDRAWN
FROM THE RECORDS OF THE
MID-CONTINENT PUBLIC LIBRARY

© 2000 by Jim Casada
All rights reserved. No portion of this publication may be reproduced or transmitted in any form or by any means, electronic or mechanical including photocopying, recording, or any information storage and retrieval systems, without permission in writing from the publisher, except by a reviewer who may quote brief passages in a critical article or review to be printed in a magazine or newspaper, or electronically transmitted on radio or television.

Edited by Brian Lovett, *Turkey & Turkey Hunting* magazine.
Book design by Allen West, Krause Publications.

Cover Credits:
Front cover photo: Fred Whitehead

Published by

krause publications

700 E. State Street • Iola, WI 54990-0001   www.krause.com

700 E. State St. • Iola, WI 54990-0001
www.krause.com

Please call or write for our free catalog of publications. Our toll-free number to place an order or to obtain a free catalog is (800) 258-0929. Please use our regular business telephone (715) 445-2214 for editorial comment and further information.
Library of Congress Catalog Number: 00-110074
ISBN: 0-87341-994-4
Printed in the United States of America

Photography by Jim Casada unless otherwise stated.

This book is dedicated to the memory of my mother,
Anna Lou Moore Casada, who passed away while it was being written.
She understood the worth of words of encouragement, knew the value of a
ready smile, and dearly loved the good Earth.

MID-CONTINENT PUBLIC LIBRARY
Blue Ridge Branch
9253 Blue Ridge Boulevard
Kansas City, Mo. 64138

BR

MID-CONTINENT PUBLIC LIBRARY

3 0001 00641063 5

4

Contents

FROM THE OUTSET, the author admired Mark Drury's innovative thinking and realized he would likely soon become a prominent, popular figure in the close-knit fraternity of turkey hunters. Pictured above are Drury, left, and the author.

Introduction

The genesis of this book dates back more than a decade, when I first met Mark Drury on a hunt at Bent Creek Lodge in Alabama. Drury had just made a big splash on the competitive turkey-calling circuit and was one of eight top-level callers who joined eight writers for the hunt. It was a writer's dream because it provided the opportunity to interview the likes of Eddie Salter, Preston Pittman, Wilbur Primos and others. Of the callers present, Drury was the only one I hadn't met. Perhaps for that reason, and because he was relatively new in terms of national renown, I arrived with no real plans to include him in my interviews. Truthfully, I doubted whether he was story material.

However, my initial exposure to Drury soon erased those preconceived notions. I found him an affable, articulate young man, whom I believed had promise in the highly competitive world he was entering. Then, through luck of the assignment draw, in which writers and hunters matched for a day afield, Drury and I were paired on the final morning of the three-day hunt. At that point, the closest I had come to killing a turkey was hearing gobbles from what might as well have been ghost birds. The only longbeards I had seen were those hanging from the rafters of the lodge porch as others reveled in success. As anyone who has experienced similar circumstances knows, you delight in hearing others recount their moments of glory. Still, deep down, you also feel the bitter bite of some envy, and at odd moments of gloominess wonder, "Why am I snakebit?"

That morning, though, as we shook off the dregs of sleep and sampled Bent Creek's solid fare, Drury lifted my slightly flagging spirits. Experienced videographer Ron Jolly, who then worked with Primos, would accompany us on the hunt. Although I knew Jolly and considered him "salt of the earth," that would have been enough to deepen my growing despair. After all, I knew too well that an additional person in the woods — not to mention the dictates connected with filming — adds exponentially to the difficulty of any turkey hunt. Then Drury smiled.

"We roosted a bird last night," he said.

Things suddenly seemed much brighter, although you can encounter many potential missteps between a roosted bird and one flopping at your feet.

Still, my hopes ran high as we drove to our destination. We had just grabbed our gear and eased the truck doors shut when the bird responded to a locator call. He was close — no more than 300 to 400 yards — and my optimism soared the way it invariably does when a ringing gobble announces the new day.

The next two hours, that optimism plummeted, almost vanished and then returned. My spirits rebounded because of a subtle yet seductive sound. It was nothing as striking as a gobble, to be sure, because the turkey went silent after he left the roost. The bird was the only game in town, though, so we waited, called occasionally and hoped. Finally, we were rewarded, albeit in a manner the uninitiated wouldn't understand or even notice.

Few things in turkey hunting can match the anxious anticipation of a hunter who hears drumming yet doesn't see the turkey. First, we heard indistinct drumming, which was so elusive none of us could be sure of it. Gradually, though, the spitting and drumming became more audible. I've only heard drumming so distinctly one other time, while hunting with Don Shipp, one of Drury's M.A.D. Calls colleagues, in Missouri. That was different, however, because the Missouri gobbler was only four to five yards away on the opposite side of a massive cottonwood. As Drury, Jolly and I later discovered, the drumming of that Alabama tom was discernible even on Jolly's tape.

For more than an hour Drury, Jolly and I sat tight in a hear-but-not-see situation. Finally, the tom gobbled again, just when the wait was about to become interminable, and a distant rumble of thunder had announced an approaching storm front. The gobble was of the shake-the-ground variety, which indicated the bird was less than 100 yards away.

Moments later, the longbeard slowly strutted into sight at about 40 yards. Almost immediately, Drury whispered, "Shoot!"

However, he didn't realize the loaner gun I was carrying had patterned miserably — so badly, in fact, that I considered it reliable at no more than 25 yards. In the ensuing 15 minutes, tension increased to an almost unbearable level as Drury repeatedly urged me to pull the trigger, and I muttered, "No," without explaining my dilemma. I'm sure he thought — he later more or less admitted as much — that he was stuck with an idiot disguised as an outdoor writer who had frozen on him. Finally, with the gobbler at 23 yards, I squeezed the trigger. The gun's shaky pattern became evident because, even at that distance, I broke the bird's wing and leg. That didn't matter, though. We had a fine longbeard with sharp, curved spurs, indicating he was at least 3 years old.

The obligatory video interviews and cutaways followed, and then I shot a couple of rolls of slide film before the heavens opened. I got a fine story from the experience. More importantly, the hunt marked the beginning of a continuing friendship with Drury. I believe only one subsequent spring has passed when Drury and I didn't hunt together. Years later, he confided that our Alabama hunt was a landmark.

"I was new in the field and quite green," he said. "But 'Cuz' Strickland, who at that time handled public relations for Mossy Oak and had set up the Bent Creek event, had given me some sound advice. He suggested I form a sound working relationship with a small cadre of writers with whom I felt comfortable and enjoyed as company."

I was one of that group, and through time, our professional relationship has become a firm friendship based on mutual respect and admiration. Seeing Drury grow as a person and hunter has been a continuing source of joy. From the outset, I admired his innovative thinking and realized he would likely soon become a prominent, popular figure in the close-knit fraternity of turkey hunters. The striking success of various M.A.D. Calls products — calls, videos and accessories — soon verified my expectations.

Somewhere along the way, Drury and I talked about doing a book that would touch on his career and detail his thoughts about hunting. From the beginning, we agreed the book should be geared toward experienced hunters, though we also hoped to appeal to newcomers. Those plans were interrupted, however, when Drury's business acumen told him it was time to sell M.A.D. Calls (he kept the video production portion) to Outland Sports.

By happy coincidence, Outland already had another call company under its umbrella. That's how Brad Harris entered the picture.

A couple of years ago, while Drury and I shared a hunting camp in Missouri with Shipp and outdoor editors Colin Moore and Brian Lovett, one of us broached the subject of the book. Drury suggested it might be a stronger work — and a fuller representation of Outland's turkey products — if it included Harris. I concurred.

Although I had spent far less time afield with Harris, I knew of his exploits and abilities. We had shared a Florida turkey camp several years before. When I arrived — a day late — he had already killed a turkey despite exceptionally tough conditions. He scored on another fine Osceola a day later. Each hunt would have left most folks shaking their head and muttering about misfortune.

Realtree founder Bill Jordan was also in that Florida camp. When Harris wasn't around one day, he said, "If I absolutely had to have a turkey, Brad Harris is one of the first folks I would turn to. I've hunted with him regularly through the years in his capacity as a member of the Realtree pro staff, and his abilities as a caller, woodsman and exceptionally gifted all-around hunter are extraordinary."

That's high praise from someone who's a talented outdoorsman and has hunted with many of the nation's finest. It made me determined to hunt with Harris, because his insight would unquestionably produce useful material for magazines or newspapers. Somehow, though, it never happened. We scheduled a hunt one year, but the weather in the Midwest turned so bad that Harris had his secretary call to suggest I cancel my trip. I agreed, and you can guess what happened. The stalled front pushed through, perfect weather followed, and gobblers celebrated with the vocal cooperativeness you rarely encounter.

Because I had enjoyed much less contact with Harris than Drury, I began to appreciate Drury's suggestion as the book took shape. Fellow writers had shared tales of positive experiences with Harris, and I was impressed by the *Lohman Guide to Successful Turkey Calling*, a book he and Monte Burch had done.

One other person loomed large in my decision to write this book: Brian Lovett, editor of *Turkey & Turkey Hunting*. Through several years of working with Lovett as editor at large for *T&TH*, I had increasingly come to respect his abilities and work ethic. This was significant, because ours could have been a writer-editor relationship fraught with peril. After all, I had been co-editor of *T&TH* for several years, and transitions in which you work with someone in a capacity you previously held can be difficult.

That hasn't been the case. Seeing Lovett grow in his knowledge and ability as a turkey hunter has given me considerable pleasure, and the opportunity to spend time together at sport shows and then hunting camps cemented our relationship. When Lovett indicated he would be willing to play a key role in overseeing the book's editorial process, that was the catalyst I needed. I had, in conjunction with my wife, Ann, written an earlier book published by Krause called *The Complete Venison Cookbook*, and it had sold well. Nonetheless, I knew this undertaking would require some in-house expertise, and Lovett was the answer.

From then, everything fell together nicely. I arranged spring hunts with Harris in Kansas and Drury in Colorado. The turkey gods shone on both excursions, thanks in large measure to my companions' expertise, and the outings produced fine gobblers. That helped for photography, although I had pretty good shots of

MARK DRURY SUGGESTED a book might be a stronger work if it included Brad Harris. Pictured here are Harris, right, and the author.

Drury from previous hunts. The trips also provided the perfect forum for extensive interviews and exchanging information. The heart of this book comes from long sessions during midday breaks, evenings after days afield and drives to and from hunting camps.

I had already formulated the book's basic outline, mostly with an eye toward covering areas significant to turkey hunters. During interviews, I tried to pick the brains of Harris and Drury about subjects covered in each chapter. The book that follows is largely the result of that. Each chapter opens with some general thoughts, based on the author's research and experience, as an introduction. Then, we get to the meat of the topic with detailed comments, occasionally spiced with anecdotes from experiences, tendered by the Outland experts.

The result is a detailed examination of the whys and wherefores of turkey hunting as seen through the eyes of two of America's highest-profile turkey hunters. There's grist here for every turkey hunter's mill. But before we get down to brass tacks, a couple of further comments are in order.

First, readers should realize that Drury and Harris are more than successful hunters and intelligent businessmen who have been able to earn a living doing what they love. They are also warm, likeable people any hard hunter would be glad to call friend. Second, I can only hope that in these pages, you will share some measure of the pleasure I have experienced getting to know and hunt with these fine fellows.

If that happens, you will be rewarded — as I have — with improved skills and savvy as a turkey hunter.

Section 1
The Quarry and the Quest

A Sport
for the Soul

Turkey hunters are a breed apart. The sport's unofficial poet laureate, Tom Kelly, recognized that in eloquent, enchanting fashion in one of turkey hunting's finest pieces of literature, *The Tenth Legion*, when he compared turkey hunters to soldiers in the Roman Empire's fabled Tenth Legion. For dedication, devotion and steadiness in even the most adverse conditions, soldiers of the Tenth Legion had no match. They were the Stonewall Brigade of the ancient world, a cult enduring through generations and the long centuries when Rome ruled the Mediterranean world and beyond. Kelly maintains that turkey hunters possess similar traits, describing them as the "spiritual descendant(s) of the original Tenth."

Anyone who has done much turkey hunting has sensed — maybe suffered — some of the feelings Kelly captured. He can depict in print what most turkey hunters feel in their hearts but find difficult or impossible to express with words. Kelly's mastery of the sport's spirit and ethos is reminiscent of the manner in which another of the sport's great scribes, Archibald Rutledge, addressed calling instruction. "Calling," he wrote, "is a thing to be learned rather than told of."

To a considerable degree, so is turkey hunting's allure. It's something you must do to appreciate, a lurking addiction that seems laughable to the uninitiated. Then, however, that unsuspecting victim innocently accepts an invitation to go turkey hunting. A few hours later, he's held in its bonds and belatedly understands the advice, "Don't get started in turkey hunting." Kelly's genius lies in appreciating these matters, and his work provides at least an inkling of why turkey hunting and turkey hunters are delightfully different.

The fullest understanding of the sport's allure, however, cannot be derived from reading. It remains the exclusive preserve of folks who take to the woods each spring full of hope. Happiness might not be their common lot — at least if you attempt to measure happiness by success — but rest assured, these are folks filled with joy. I realize I'm preaching to the choir, but sometimes it doesn't hurt to remember that dead turkeys don't always define hunting pleasure.

In fact, you'll find few of us who haven't spent sleepless nights, tossing and turning, and mired in the misery of miscues remembered and relived. Our nightmares might revolve around a missed shot or merely a minor mistake. Perhaps they focus on a momentary opportunity that slipped away, or a happenstance occurrence that left us helpless and forlorn. That's the nature of turkey hunting.

Ponder the almost mythical qualities hunters associate with the turkey. One description of the bird's wariness compares it with the white-tailed deer. "A deer sees a distant man and thinks he is a stump," it says, but, "The turkey sees a stump and thinks it is a man." Another bit of folk wisdom deals with the bird's awesome vision and hearing. It says, "A turkey can see a flea scratch itself at 400 yards and hear a mosquito buzz at 800 yards."

Obviously, those are overstatements, but they send a clear message: Hunters like dealing with an adversary they have endowed with almost supernatural qualities. Incidentally, these supposed attributes of turkeys — there's a fair share of truth in such descriptions — also serve as explanations or excuses for failure, and failure is an integral, important part of the sport's lure and lore.

I know of no other type of hunting or fishing in which participants regularly revel in tales of woe to such an extent. Sure, anglers talk about "the one that got away," but they don't take 15 minutes to describe their distress, followed by 30 more minutes of analysis of what went wrong. In turkey hunting, however, such lengthy tales are common. Amazingly, other hunters listen, and not merely out of politeness. They are enthralled and entranced, fellow prisoners with the storyteller in a world turned upside down. It's a world where the pain of hunts gone wrong somehow equates to pleasure, and where a bird with a brain the size of an underdeveloped Georgia peanut regularly bests the creature that supposedly sits atop the evolutionary ladder.

When you try to assess or explain why any sane person would endure

Jennifer Pillath

THE FULLEST UNDERSTANDING of the sport's allure cannot be derived from reading. It remains the exclusive preserve of folks who take to the woods each spring full of hope.

Brad Harris

THE DELIGHTFUL DISEASE sometimes called turkey fever flourishes like never before because turkeys have become so plentiful and widespread.

such self-imposed agony, it can be difficult to find a logical answer. After all, the sport carries the heavy baggage of apprehension, a haunting premonition that somehow, some way, something will go wrong. Worse, it usually does.

That's why my turkey hunting mentor, Parker Whedon, a gifted hunter whose insights into the sport match his skills, said, "The only certainty in turkey hunting is uncertainty."

Much of turkey hunting's allure derives from its great difficulty. The breathless anticipation, frequent failures and unpredictability of the quarry try the patience of the most steadfast hunters. Still, those characteristics of turkeys and the hunt also capture the human spirit and imagination. A few days ago, I reviewed some writing that described my earliest turkey hunting experiences, and a phrase caught my eye. I had written that from my first hunt, the turkey "had laid hold on a corner of my soul." That hasn't changed in the subsequent decades, except the hold has grown stronger as its roots extended to the depths of my being.

The same sense of awe and wonder became clear as I hunted with and interviewed the two fellows whose wisdom comprises the heart of this book. Mark Drury and Brad Harris realize they had the good fortune to grow up in areas with turkeys. That meant they "lost their souls" early. That wasn't my lot, because turkeys had all but disappeared from North Carolina's Great Smoky Mountains during my boyhood in the late 1940s and 1950s. Because I couldn't hunt turkeys, you might say I had a deprived childhood. Mind you, though, I've been trying to make up for it since.

So have millions of other hunters, thanks largely to the great bird's comeback. We'll take a detailed look at that in Chapter 3. For now, suffice to say, the delightful disease sometimes called turkey fever flourishes like never before, and it has because turkeys have become so plentiful and widespread.

The lives of Harris and Drury almost parallel the era of turkey restoration, which means they have been blessed. Their respective careers also exemplify the sport's changing face, one that has seen rapid expansion of hunting knowledge and willingness to share wisdom. That was seldom found in earlier generations. In the first half of the 20th century, turkey hunters were typically secretive to the extreme. The essence of this book results from the opposite. It features two fairly young but seasoned hunters joining a writer to share their knowledge.

Drury and Harris admit they have miles to run and years of lessons yet to learn. However, the value of experience — especially blended with astute observation and a willingness to probe new areas of knowledge — means hunters should hear and heed their voices. Also, as we'll see in the next chapter, Drury and Harris relish every aspect of turkey hunting — even as they revere the noble bird that makes it possible.

Perhaps no one better captured those qualities than Rutledge. In his sage, inimitable fashion, the man whose sons called him "Old Flintlock" used overtones similar to those of Kelly. He also depicted turkey hunters as a special, close-knit fraternity. Who can resist the words and wisdom of a man who named his box call "Miss Seduction" as his writing echoes back from the darkening corridors of the sport's yesteryears. "Some men," he wrote, "are mere hunters; others are turkey hunters."

THE ELUSIVE, ULTIMATELY UNATTAINABLE holy grail of turkey hunting perfection mesmerizes us and makes the continuing study — striving to learn and improve — so joyous.

His succinct words recognized that for him, and countless others, turkey hunting became a mystical experience. Incredibly, Rutledge hunted turkeys during eight decades, mostly in his home state of South Carolina but also Pennsylvania. During that long career — in an era when turkey numbers were at historic lows — Old Flintlock killed almost 400 turkeys.

With that to his credit, Rutledge must be reckoned a true old master. However, according to his standards of judgment, no man can really approach mastery in turkey hunting.

Near the peak of his career, reminiscing about countless wonderful days during quests for gobblers, Flintlock acknowledged as much.

"Turkey hunting has been with me a kind of religion ever since a hatchet was a hammer," he wrote, "and perhaps I have learned a little of the art. Yet even after almost a half-century of hunting of the noblest game bird that graces America's wild, I am going to confess that I am still in the kindergarten; and I doubt if any human being ever acquires a complete education in this high art."

Turkey hunting provides a constant reminder of the thought offered by Horace Kephart, a superb woodsman sometimes remembered as the "Dean of American Campers."

"In the school of the outdoors," he wrote, "there is no graduation day."

The elusive, ultimately unattainable holy grail of turkey hunting perfection mesmerizes us and makes the continuing study — striving to learn and improve — so joyous.

As turkey hunters, we know and appreciate that our pursuit is a sport for the soul.

IN 1989, MARK, LEFT, AND TERRY DRURY launched Drury Outdoors, a video-production business. These turkeys were killed in May 1990, and were the first gobblers the pair filmed.

Roots
The Hunters' Backgrounds

The making of a hunter, especially when the process begins in youth, involves a continually unfolding marvel. Delightful discoveries of self and the hunter's ethos join with the wonder every sportsman experiences at milestones such as their first turkey.

Special hunts provide memories for the mind's vaults, waiting for years or decades to be resurrected and enjoyed again. A hunting apprenticeship forges friendships and strengthens family ties, because it's rare that a budding hunter goes alone. He has mentors to guide him and buddies to share his bliss. If he is blessed, this will occur during youth.

Robert Ruark, who I believe was America's greatest outdoor scribe, dedicated his enchanting, enduring 1957 book *The Old Man and the Boy* to his grandfathers, father and "all the honorary uncles, black and white, who took me to raise." We might wish to be so blessed, because, as Ruark mentions in his "Author's Note" in the work, "Anybody who reads this book is bound to realize that I had a real fine time as a kid."

The same can be said about Brad Harris and Mark Drury. Better yet — and this sharply contrasts Ruark's checkered career — they continue to have real fine times as adults.

Folks speak about being "as American as baseball and apple pie," but that could be said of growing up in a rural setting, loving the land and learning to hunt at an early age. The people involved in this book enjoyed such circumstances. Memories of hunting and fishing in and near tiny Bryson City, in the heart of North Carolina's Great Smokies, are among my earliest and fondest childhood recollections. Bryson City's population in the 1960 census, when I finished high school, was about 1,800. Three decades later, the population was 1,450. For someone who places great value on solitude and elbow room, that's progress.

Born the better part of a generation after me, Harris and Drury are staunch sons of the American heartland, having grown up in game-rich Missouri. In some senses, we represent a world that somehow seems to be gradually slipping away. That's sad, because ours is a world where family ties, the value of hard work and a belief in a connection to the natural world loom large. However, those virtues, long heralded as the essence of what it meant to be an American, seem increasingly elusive. They seem fated to fade in the face of assaults on gun ownership, a continuing increase in one-parent families, burgeoning populations and urbanization, and decreasing numbers of folks who consider hard work and solid citizenship matters of pride.

For people who hunt and still cling to such values, there's a message. We'll return to it in this book's final chapter, where we ponder what tomorrow might bring. For the moment, though, note how Drury and Harris' youths molded and chiseled them into modern versions of the woodsmen and hunting heroes who dominated our folklore — Daniel Boone, Davy Crockett, Jim Bowie, Alvin York, the mountain men, the plains scouts and the Over the Mountain Boys, hunters who helped turn the tide of the American Revolution. Drury and Harris come from the same cloth, and each might be called — to borrow the simple yet expressive title of one of Archibald Rutledge's books — "An American Hunter."

The shaping and structuring of these hunters began early, and their roots — with Drury and Harris serving as guides — tells us as much. The proverb that maintains, "The child is the father of the man," holds true for them. They began turkey hunting while young, nurturing their skills and appreciation of woodcraft. To retrace those youthful footsteps is to tread paths of wonder. It also provides a necessary backdrop for everything that follows. Here, mostly in their words shared in spring turkey camps, is a look at the Outland experts' backgrounds.

MARK DRURY

"I was born in Perryville, Mo., and grew up in the town of Bloomsdale in the same state," Drury said. "Bloomsdale was a tiny town of about 400 people, and my father, Ralph, and uncle, Marvin, owned a construction company there. By good fortune, my childhood home was located so that from the house to the Mississippi River, about four miles away, there was a block of mature forest. This large, wild area held turkeys, so I was exposed

DRURY OUTDOORS HAS BRANCHED OUT into whitetail hunting, but turkey hunting footage paved the way. Turkey videos continue to be an important part of the business. Above, Mark Drury sets up to film Tad Brown.

to them at an early age."

Along with what was almost a wilderness for a playground and back yard, Drury was also greatly influenced by membership in the Boy Scouts of America.

"I became very involved in Cub Scouts when I was old enough, and from that point until my teen-age years, there was almost constant scouting-related outdoors activities of some sort," he said. "I earned a bevy of merit badges and achieved the rank of Eagle Scout in February of my eighth-grade year."

Those familiar with scouting realize achieving that difficult, demanding rank at such a young age is extraordinary.

"My scouting experiences gave me a great deal of joy, and looking back on them, I realize just how much they meant to me," he said. "They were an ideal introduction to the world of the outdoors."

Drury also spent lots of time alone in the woods. Perhaps these long hours of solitude unconsciously helped prepare him as a turkey hunter. The title of a 1987 Kenny Morgan book, *Turkey Hunting — A One Man Game*, sums things up: A dyed-in-the-wool turkey hunter might relish good company and cherish sporting friendships, but he must also be comfortable and content going solo in the wild.

"I was the youngest of five children," Drury said, "and I was by myself a lot. Dad seldom hunted, although my brother, Terry, was an avid outdoorsman. However, Terry is 10 years older than me, and that's a wide enough gap in childhood to make a real difference."

As a young boy, Drury box-trapped rabbits and hunted squirrels frequently with his Grandpa Ritter.

"I was always close to my maternal grandfather," he said, showing how youngsters can skip a generation to link hands with old-timers in a tested, timeless partnership.

Drury smiled as he reminisced about Grandpa Ritter and how his mother viewed family influence in his growth as a hunter.

"Mom has always been fond of saying, 'You get your love of hunting from my side of the family,' and she's right," he said. "She taught me how to skin squirrels and rabbits."

It's apparent Drury's mother wisely recognized that a lad absorbed in nature was far removed from the temptations that led to what was then called juvenile delinquency.

Another incident from Drury's childhood has humorous overtones.

"I box-trapped a rabbit, and it was still alive," he said. "Dad said, 'I'll bet you can't catch it again.' Then he took a can of spray paint, marked the cottontail and turned it loose despite my protests. Sure enough, I didn't catch it again, or if I did, all the paint was gone."

Drury continued his development as a sportsman in high school.

"It was at the beginning of my high school years that I really got into turkey hunting," he said.

An insightful teacher, recognizing a subject that would produce maximum effort, let Drury research and write a report on turkeys and turkey hunting.

"My Uncle Marvin was a real inspiration when it came to turkey hunting," Drury said. "During grammar school, when he got his bird — and he almost always did — he would even bring it to school for a session of show-and-tell. Earlier this year (Spring 2000), I had the opportunity to experience some of the delight Marvin must have known. I took a turkey I had killed down to the preschool group my daughter, Taylor, is a part of, and gave her class the same sort of performance I enjoyed as a child."

When Drury reached high school, Uncle Marvin evidently figured Drury was ready to hunt turkeys because he began offering tips and suggestions about how to deal with gobblers. Progress came slowly, although Drury gained an appreciation of how tough turkey hunting could be, along with early lessons in patience.

"I started by hunting from a blind," he said, "and I knew almost nothing. In fact, I went turkeyless for three years, even though I hunted hard.

"Every day during the season when I didn't have to be in school, Mom would drive me to where I planned to hunt and drop me off. She would be back to pick me up when legal hunting hours ended."

Obviously, she was as supportive a mother as a budding hunter could want.

"During that period, I had lots of encounters — all of them unsuccessful," Drury said. "Finally, though, when I was 17 and a senior in high school, I got my first turkey. It came after a great deal of effort, and long before that moment, one thing had become clear: I realized that I needed to be a better caller, although looking back, my problems went well beyond poor calling."

However, Drury's focus on improved calling reveals an aspect of his personality that proved critical years later.

"I was analytical from an early age," he said, which lies at the heart of his call-making success.

Back then, though, Drury was simply determined to become a better caller. He began to attend and enter calling contests.

"When I was 16 years old, I competed in a calling contest in Festus, Mo., and placed third," he said. "With that, I was on my way as a competition caller."

He found a running buddy in Greg Jaegers, and the pair became inseparable. Also, as they began entering contests, Drury began experiencing the caring and sharing that insiders say typifies the competitive turkey calling world.

"Steve Stoltz, Jeff Probst and everyone took me under their wings to some degree right from the outset," he said.

Meanwhile, Drury's true breakthrough came during his senior year.

"Bill Martin, my coach and physics teacher, was the man who really taught me how to hunt turkeys," he said, "forgiving my tardiness to my first-period physics class almost every day during turkey hunting season."

Martin accepted that and gave Drury invaluable tips and pointers that only a veteran hunter could provide.

"My first turkey was a jake," Drury said. "He came to me giving slow lost-yelps all the way, and after the shot, I was almost beside myself with excitement."

His second turkey, however, killed that same spring, increased his passion and proved he had, to some degree, arrived as a hunter.

"My second bird came after one of those hunts that are sometimes described as classic," he said. "I worked him for two hours, and when he eventually came in range and I made a clean shot, I found I had killed a trophy. He was a big, sharp-spurred bronze-phase gobbler — a lovely turkey. Unfortunately, despite my ecstasy, I didn't really know what I had, and I didn't get the tom mounted. I've periodically regretted that since."

Those turkeys proved to be a turning point in Drury's life.

"From there on, I was really into turkeys," he said. "I was immersed, going to calling contests every time I could. In fact, I was so absorbed that turkeys even took precedence over girls."

Maybe, but not to absolute absorption. As we talked during a mid-May morning, Drury temporarily reminisced about the romance of his life, mentioning that his first date with Tracy — now his wife — happened May 10, 1985.

"Of course," he said, "that was the weekend after the season ended."

They married Oct. 21, 1987.

After high school, Drury enrolled at the University of Missouri at Rolla. He subsequently transferred and completed his bachelor's studies, earning a degree in industrial technology at Southeast Missouri State. Meanwhile, immediately preceding his marriage, he began calling competitively at the national level.

"I won my first state contest in 1987, the Tennessee Open," he said. "The same year, I placed second in the Levi Garrett National Finals."

The next year, he went on his first hunt outside of Missouri.

"Other things started clicking," he said. "In 1989, Terry and I started Drury Outdoors and launched the video-production effort we still work with today. That was Terry's first year to hunt turkeys. The same year also brought my first really big contest victory. In February, at Natchez, Miss., I won the World Natural Voice contest. Preston Pittman, who was already a legend, finished second or third in that contest. He also whispered congratulations to me as I approached the stage to receive the trophy, saying, 'No one will ever take this away from you.'"

Pittman also did something more concrete.

"He introduced me to Toxey Haas and Ronnie 'Cuz' Strickland of Mossy Oak," Drury said. "He said to them, 'You'd better sign him up. This boy's going places.' I got to know Toxey, and a couple of months later, spent some time with him and his wife, Diane, while visiting the Mossy Oak headquarters in West Point, Miss."

That occurred during spring break from college in Drury's junior year.

Haas convinced Drury to join the Mossy Oak pro staff and urged Cecil Carder of Advanced Marketing Specialities, an agency that worked for the camo maker, to hire him.

"I signed on, and for the next nine years worked as a representative for Cecil while simultaneously growing the video business," he said. "Our timing with the videos was good, and from the outset, our productions sold well."

Drury Outdoors has branched out into whitetail hunting, but turkey hunting footage paved the way. Turkey videos continue to be an important part of the business.

"Our first six videos, beginning with *King of Spring* and *The Sound of Spring — A Video Dictionary*, which were released in 1990, were about wild turkeys," Drury said. "Toxey Haas encouraged my work as a videographer, and those early years of video work also found me on the road quite a bit. I was selling as a rep, marketing the videos and also started doing some in-store promotions and seminars. That experience really helped me refine my speaking skills and improved the way I worked with the public."

The late 1980s and early 1990s must have been heady for Drury. He won the World Natural Voice Calling Championship three consecutive years — 1989, 1990 and 1991 — and then, as he said, "I quit while I was ahead."

In 1992, he won the World Championship, and the next year won the World Team Championship with Stoltz.

"Steve also won the World Championship that year," Drury said, "and I placed second. Clearly, it was a great World for us."

Only three years later, after being crowned King of Calls in a 1996 competition that required entrants to use all the basic types of calls, Drury left contest calling. In less than a decade, he had made his way to the top, and new challenges awaited him. He had expanded in the video business with the 1992 release of *Monster Bucks*, the first of a continuing series. In 1993, he launched M.A.D. Calls, the name of which is taken from his initials.

29

"It was almost overwhelming," Drury said. "I convinced Tad Brown, a fellow Missourian and good hunting buddy, to join M.A.D. Calls as manager, and in 1994, we were ready to offer our first product to the public."

At the Shooting, Hunting and Outdoor Trade, or SHOT, Show that year, M.A.D. introduced the Callmaker, which let hunters craft their own diaphragm calls. The slogan that marked the device's advent was vintage Drury: "Adding New Technology to an Old Tradition." According to Drury, the product resulted from his competitive call-making background, and again, the timing was right.

Most stores that carried Drury's videos also stocked the M.A.D. Calls line.

"We actually made money that year," Drury said, "something that seldom happens with the launch of a new business. We were off and running."

After that, one new, noteworthy product followed another. If you look at the history of M.A.D. Calls, you soon realize part of the game plan is to offer one item each year that grabs the turkey hunting public's attention.

After the Callmaker, M.A.D. introduced a locator call named Dead Silence.

"I got the concept from Paul Rishel," Drury said. "He was our biggest customer."

That was M.A.D.'s first venture into the high-frequency call field. Next came a friction call, 1996's Super Aluminator (again, notice the knack for names). Considerable research preceded the call, during which Drury tested various calls on a spectrograph to determine their frequency.

I had a small part in that research. I remember sitting with Drury in a motel room somewhere in the Midwest, with a spring snowstorm bearing down, running every wingbone I had while Drury recorded and made notes on the calls' frequencies. During previous trips, he had noticed I enjoyed success locating birds with the wingbone, and believed frequency was a critical factor.

Although call-makers had previously used aluminum in friction calls — Dick Kirby of Quaker Boy used it years earlier — the Aluminator and its high, almost squeaky tone garnered the public's attention. Continuing with the high-frequency concept, M.A.D. introduced a waterproof box call, the Super Carbonator, in 1997, and the Carbonator II and Pure Crystal friction call in 1998.

"I was always trying to run at least a year ahead of the competition,"

Drury said, "and we were constantly growing all the while. During the middle of the 1990s, I also made a real point of establishing contact with a group of well-established writers and hunting with them regularly. Cuz Strickland had advised me to do this, and this led to close professional relationships with a number of top writers: Kathy Etling, Brian Lovett, Jerome Robinson, Bryce Towsley, Mike Hanback and, of course, you.

"I learned from writers, and there were also a bunch of folks from other segments of the outdoor industry who taught me. Also, I made my share of mistakes and learned from them. Mossy Oak's Bob Dixon once advised me to take a negative and turn it into a positive. That's something I have tried to do."

At times, all of this was almost overwhelming, and Drury said he worried about not having enough time for himself or with his family.

That unquestionably figured into the mix when, in October 1997, he sold M.A.D. Calls to Outland Sports.

"Outland was in an acquisition mode, and Brad Harris had talked with me," Drury said. "We were red hot at the time, and it was an ideal opportunity for me to make a move. Of course, Outland only acquired M.A.D. Calls. Drury Outdoors, the video production part of the operation, and the place where Terry and I got started stayed in our hands."

Coming under Outland's umbrella made little difference for M.A.D. In 1999, after considerable analysis of chokes, forcing cones and other shotgun-patterning factors, the company introduced the M.A.D. Max line of chokes. In 2000, the company introduced the Super Titanium call. In 2001, hunters can look for locator calls with cherry-wood barrels.

"All are loud and high-pitched," Drury said "and they have the aesthetic appeal that's important to many hunters."

Drury continues to work on ads with catchy slogans and a visual appeal that grabs magazine readers. Also, he's busier than ever with video work.

"With new hunters constantly coming into the sport, we started our Mastery series with them in mind," he said. "In 1999, we brought out four instructional tapes — on mouth calls, locator calls, friction calls and one with general coverage. A tape on box calls is in the works.

What does the future hold for Drury?

"That's anybody's guess," he said. "The hunting world has treated me exceptionally well, financially and otherwise, and I'm still young with lots of ideas and maybe even some dreams to pursue. For now, though, I'm happy to be a part of the Outland team, to be making videos and spending time doing what I love best."

BRAD HARRIS

"I was born on June 29, 1957 in Bonne Terre, Mo.," Harris said.

Somehow, the name of that town, which means good earth in French, seems appropriate for someone who has spent his life in close, intimate contact with the natural world.

Harris grew up in Desloges, Mo., and proudly proclaimed, "I have been a Missouri resident all my life." Raised in a sporting family that lived for outdoor pursuits, Harris was one of nine children.

"All four of my brothers hunted," he said. "Dad started them, as he did me, on rabbits and squirrels. We were taught the lessons of safety first, and our father always emphasized the value of being in the outdoors and constantly reminded us that it was a privilege to be able to hunt."

Then, the senior Harris turned the boys loose.

"Once we had been trained as hunters and sportsmen, he had enough faith in us to let us hunt on our own," Harris said. "Also, Mom and Dad firmly believed that being outdoors hunting and fishing was a good place for youngsters."

The family lived on a small farm, which was ideally situated for youngsters who loved the outdoors.

"There were two rivers nearby," Harris said, "and hunting land was available and accessible. Dad wasn't a turkey hunter, but he was a keen bird hunter (in those days, bird hunting meant quail hunting, and quail were *the* game bird in the eyes of most who hunted them). Everybody in the family hunted deer, but it was my grandfather who guided me through my early experiences in turkey hunting."

Harris' grandfather belonged to the old school, which knew the difficulties of dealing with turkeys when they were scarce. In those days, most turkey hunters reluctantly shared knowledge — if at all.

"I loved to listen to Grandpa tell tales," Harris said, "and our Sunday afternoon sessions were almost a ritual. It was a part of the week I always looked forward to with eagerness."

Harris' grandfather was also a talented fiddle player, and sometimes the fireside or back-porch sessions mixed music-making with tale-telling. One of the stories Harris and his grandfather cherished dealt with the grandfa-

HUNTING WAS A WAY of life for the Harris family. Pete Harris, Brad's father, and his Grandpa Farmer hold birds killed by Brad and his brother John in 1979.

Brad Harris

ther's first experience with fall turkeys.

"Grandpa was fascinated by the first set of turkey tracks he ever saw," Harris said. "After locating the tracks, he spent days in the woods trying to get up with them. He even got lost during the process, but eventually he located the flock and killed a bird."

Harris heard that tale when he was 6 or 7, and it planted a seed. It took several years to sprout and begin growing, but through his preteen years, even as he hunted small game, Harris said he had "turkeys on the mind."

Harris first hunted turkeys in 1971.

"Turkeys were still not particularly plentiful," he said, "and few folks hunted them or knew much about them. But I did know a few nearby landowners who had a few birds, and I was able to get permission to hunt."

Harris' best buddy, Charley Zobrisky, lived four miles away.

"Our favorite hunting spot was White Oak Creek, which was an additional eight miles from Charley's house," he said.

Zobrisky's mother dropped them off there before daylight.

"Usually, we heard turkeys gobble, although we didn't really know what to do and didn't kill any," he said. "Still, the gobbling seized my soul, and it still does. Then, as now, there's nothing quite like being in the woods on a spring morning with the woods awakening, and hearing a tom declare his dominion."

It was a time of wonder for the adolescents.

"Those trips to White Oak Creek were our equivalent of an African safari," Harris said with a laugh. "We enjoyed them in the way only two boys being in a place they love can. We would separate when we entered the woods, and normally hunted until about 9 a.m. Then, we would be homeward bound, usually managing to get a ride with a farmer."

Like Drury, Harris' early years were learning experiences.

"I went turkey hunting every chance for three years without killing a bird," he said. "There were encounters but no closure."

Harris believes he was too cautious.

"I had gotten so caught up in not making mistakes — and I made lots of them — that in calling, in particular, I was much too conservative," he said. "But I kept plugging away, and it seemed like every time despair would begin to set in, something would happen to lift my spirits."

A good example of this occurred when Harris inadvertently set up before daylight within 30 yards of a gobbler.

"That was my first really meaningful encounter," he said, "and I was mesmerized. The gobbler finally flew off to the next ridge, but for a long time after that, all I had to do to have the itch was to think about that tom and the way I could see him profiled against the sky with his beard hanging down."

In 1973, Harris and Zobrisky got their driver's licenses, which made turkey hunting somewhat easier.

"We would hunt every chance, and if the turkeys didn't work or were quiet, we would usually go fishing in nearby rivers or ponds," he said. "There was always plenty to do, and through time, we encountered what few turkey hunters there were.

"We always asked permission to hunt, and it was usually granted. Turkeys were spotty, but the folks who had land turkeys used — even if only periodically — would tell us. We tried a lot of places, but most of our efforts were on one three-mile stretch of White Oak Creek. We got to know it mighty well, and it was the most predictable place to hear turkeys."

Harris' epiphany as an emerging turkey hunter came when he obtained and learned to use two homemade calls. One was given to him by Dean

Qualls, the best-known hunter in the area.

"He was a hunter ahead of his time in some senses," Harris said. "He was an avid bow-hunter for deer, and hunted turkeys with success from Missouri's first spring season."

Qualls had a son who was close friends with Harris' brothers, and Harris used this to pick Qualls' brain.

"Dean made me my first diaphragm call," he said. "He used two lead washers, surgical tape and a condom. He also taught me how to use it."

About that time, Harris' grandfather gave him a lovingly fashioned box call, which Harris still believes — even after he accidentally cracked it — is one of the best-sounding calls he has used.

"Obtaining those calls and learning to use them, along with another break-through, really got me going," he said. "It was my good fortune that Dean Qualls needed a place to hunt. I had one, and when I told him, 'I can't kill 'em,' he agreed to accompany me. In fact, his exact words were, 'I'll show you how.'"

When Harris picked up Qualls a few mornings later, he assumed the veteran would call and that he would finally have a chance to kill a turkey. To his chagrin, when they reached their hunting area, Qualls said, "Which way do you want to go? I'll go the other way."

Deeply disappointed but not knowing what else to do, Harris walked away alone. Worse, later that morning, he heard a shot and learned Qualls had indeed, in a fashion, shown him how to kill a turkey. Harris still chuckles about how, through his inflated expectations, he had been snookered.

"To Dean's credit," he said, "we went again the next day. I observed every-thing he did closely, listening to his calling and watching his woodsmanship. I learned more in that one hunt than I had the three previous years. Dean was not aggressive by today's standards, and certainly not by the way I hunt, but he understood turkeys and provided me with invaluable information."

Harris' first turkey came soon afterward.

"I was 16, and Grandpa's box call brought the bird to me," he said. "It was an unusual hunt in many ways. It was 8:30 a.m., and I heard a distant gobble."

Harris maneuvered to get higher and closer to the turkey.

"I heard him gobbling as I went, but when I got close, the turkey shut up," he said. "Then I called, and he cut me off with a gobble. I didn't see him until he was within 25 yards, and he was only 20 yards away when I hammered him."

As Harris stood over his first turkey, almost overwhelmed by the emotional rush, he heard someone whistle on the other side of the creek.

"It turns out the fellow had been working the bird for an hour, but I had no way of knowing that, and was in a place where I was supposed to be," he said. "What that did was give me confidence, because I realized I had called in a turkey while unknowingly competing with another hunter. From that point, I became much more aggressive, and my approach to turkey hunting has always been one of making things happen — of building a fire in the bird."

That turkey also fueled a flame in Harris, which has burned brightly since.

"I immediately realized I wanted and needed to be a better caller," he said. "In 1976-'77, I started entering calling competitions. From that time on, I thought and breathed turkeys, and the contest circuit helped me a lot as a hunter. At that time, almost all the competition callers were hunters first and competitors second. To a man, they were willing to talk about hunting and offer their insights, and I probed for information at every chance."

Harris also immersed himself in the sport in other ways.

"I started buying calls," he said, "and I still have some old Ben Lee and Penn's Woods calls that are probably collectors' items today, not to mention a 33-rpm record."

Eventually, Harris' competition-calling experiences led him to the business side of turkey hunting.

"From when I first started down to 1978, I called in all the local Missouri contests," he said. "There were usually just eight or nine entrants. I enjoyed quite a bit of success and won a number of local contests. Then in 1978 or 1979, I entered the Missouri State competition and won second place in the contest as well as first place in owl hooting."

He owled with his natural voice, something few contestants did at that time.

During the next few years, Harris won many awards for owl hooting and turkey calling.

"Ray Eye was my main competition, but there were other fine callers in Missouri as well," he said.

The Mid-America Open was held in Kansas City in 1980, and Harris and several hunting buddies entered the event.

"I was scared to death," he said, "for in my eyes, this was the sure-enough

BRAD HARRIS' FIRST experience with a gobbler mesmerized him, and he soon became absorbed in calling and woodsmanship. His first bow-kill came in 1977, left. He was soon hunting for gobblers across the nation with other turkey fanatics. Below from left are Harris, Chris Yeoman and Monte Burch in South Dakota.

Brad Harris

37

big time."

Dressed in old Army camo, which for him was then standard attire, Harris conquered his nerves, placing third in the Open and winning the owling contest.

Bill Harper, who had recently bought Lohman Calls, was the master of ceremonies.

"He liked my owling and introduced himself afterward," Harris said. "We got to talking, and he asked me, 'Who do you call for?' I didn't really know what he meant and replied, 'I just hunt.'"

Harper explained that he would like for Harris to use his calls, but it didn't dawn on Harris what was happening.

"I thought he wanted me to sell calls," Harris said.

Instead, Harris left Kansas City loaded with turkey calls and a crow call.

"All the way home, I was like a kid at Christmas going through my treasures," he said. "I used the calls and worked to improve my calling with them."

Soon afterward, Harris won a local contest using Lohman calls, and Harper began to ask him to do seminars.

"All of this sort of came together for me in the late 1970s and early 1980s," Harris said, "and then Bill Harper asked me to make a tape on locating. He said he would pay me to come to his headquarters in Neosho, put me up in a motel and even take me goose hunting."

Harris harbored a somewhat shy country boy's reservations about the enterprise, but the offer of goose hunting — something he knew little about — proved too tempting.

The sessions resulted in *Owl Hooting and Turkey Locating*, the industry's first tape about locator calling.

"I was intimidated by the whole undertaking," Harris said. "Yet even today, two decades later, I occasionally have people come up to me and say, 'I learned to owl hoot from your tape.' I always have a good feeling when someone does that."

Harris left Neosho with much to ponder.

"Bill Harper really knew goose hunting, and from that point on, I was an avid waterfowler," he said. "Also, I liked him, and before I started back home, he asked me to join him the next spring (1981) at a hunting camp he had at Lake of the Ozarks. I was to help him by doing some guiding, as well as having a chance to hunt turkeys on my own. I was delighted to accept, and

I guess you could say that at that point I became a genuine Lohman pro staffer."

The camp included a major industry buyer and Johnny Morris of Bass Pro Shops fame.

"The first morning, I took the buyer out," Harris said. "It was absolutely miserable: cold, misting rain and nothing was happening. Finally, after covering a lot of ground and doing a lot of calling, I struck a bird. He responded well, and I got him within 14 yards. The hunter became so excited or agitated he wouldn't shoot, so when the turkey started to leave, I killed it."

Harris almost immediately realized the heat of the moment had gotten the better of his judgment, and he began to apologize profusely. However, the buyer was delighted.

"He confessed that he had frozen up, and bragged on me to Johnny Morris when we got back to camp," he said. "I guided for Mr. Morris the next spring, and he really helped get me going in some ways by speaking well of me to other folks."

After Harris' second spring of guiding at Lake of the Ozarks, Harper approached him about moving to Neosho to run the Lohman shop and help develop new products.

"I had been working in an open pit-mining operation since 1976," Harris said, "and was already married and had two children. The miners happened to be on strike at the time, so I agreed — although with some real reservations — to go for an interview."

Harper introduced Harris to Jack Lohman, whose father had started the business in 1937.

"Jack was still involved in an advisory capacity," Harris said, "and he knew a lot about woodworking and the way calls were made. He was also a great caller and in particular could run a crow call like no one else I've heard."

They toured Lohman's 5,000-square-foot building in Neosho, met the operation's 17 employees, looked at the call-making machines and discussed the business. At the end of the tour, Harris said, Lohman turned to Harper and said, "I think the kid can do it." Soon afterward, Harper made him a formal offer.

"It was a difficult decision," Harris said. "I talked it over with Teri (his wife) and then with Dad. After hearing me out, my father gave me some sound advice: 'Son, this is a good opportunity, and the timing is right. You can always come back home if things don't work out.' That was all it took to make up my mind."

In December 1983, Harris went to work for Lohman Calls. For the first two months, he commuted to Neosho and spent 14 hours a day in the shop learning how the machines worked.

"Jack Lohman, as honest and straightforward a guy as you could want, helped me tremendously," he said.

The first four years, Harris did it all.

"I ran the shop, oversaw production and the machines, worked on filling orders and served as a boss," he said. "It was really tough for a while, but there were some real pleasures as well. I got to hunt quite a bit and began to meet and hunt with some writers."

One of the first was veteran scribe and Missouri resident Monte Burch.

"Monte gave me some great guidance on how to act, deal with the public and present myself," Harris said. "Similarly, Jack Nelson, Lohman's sales manager, taught me the details of the business from the standpoint of dealing with big customers."

Harris said he was blessed by deciding to join Lohman Calls.

"The timing was right," he said. "Turkey populations were exploding, and of course that meant hunter numbers and the demand for products did the same thing."

Harris has been a fixture in the business for two decades. During that time, he expanded his horizons by becoming a Realtree pro staffer, and has made his mark in the turkey world and other facets of hunting.

His original job involved product development, and his influence has been significant. Probably his most notable product breakthrough was that he designed and developed the first grunt call for deer hunters, something almost every deer hunter carries afield. Another of his noteworthy products was the Turkey Tracer, a slate call with a walnut base featuring slots that produced different sounds and restricted striker motion, simplifying its operation.

"It was introduced about a decade or so ago," Harris said, "and for a couple of years, it was the top-selling slate on the market."

Harris also helped develop a two-chambered box call using walnut. That resulted from watching Merriam's react to calling from great distances and, reminiscent of Drury, noticing how birds responded to high-end sounds.

"That was a real revelation to me," Harris said.

Harris also designed the Hot Single diaphragm, a single-reed call

ONE OF BRAD HARRIS' NOTEWORTHY products is the Turkey Tracer, a slate call with a walnut base featuring slots that produce different sounds and restrict striker motion, simplifying its operation.

designed for easy use, soft sounds and a higher pitch.

"In truth," he said, "I have had a part in development of almost all the new products from Lohman and now Outland. Part of the evaluation process — before anything goes on the market — is my testing the item and offering input. Before I give final approval, I want to work with it, and that is best done in real-life hunting situations."

Although Harris is no longer a regular contest competitor, he retains his touch. At the National Rifle Association's 2000 convention, he entered an unusual contest in which competitors called for predators, turkeys, deer and elk. He won, demonstrating what anyone who has been afield with him realizes — Harris is a hunter for all seasons.

Still, turkeys remain his first love and greatest passion.

Brian Lovett

42

A Wary, Worthy Adversary

A long, heavy bookcase crafted from solid black walnut rests just steps from the desk where I write these words. I treasure it for two reasons. It was lovingly fashioned by the talented hands of my late father-in-law, Ernest Fox, soon after I had taken his only child from him. That makes the bookcase near and dear to me. Because of that personal link, it's a fitting repository for my collection of books, pamphlets and other material relating to turkeys.

The collection serves as a testament to one man's fixation. In a wider sense, however, it speaks about the obsession the turkey can bring to a hunter's life. Almost from when I began hunting turkeys, I have collected the sport's literature and other related memorabilia. As a result, I have more than 150 books or pamphlets that deal with turkey hunting, along with scores of scientific studies and hundreds of old magazines with articles about the sport. Printed material forms the primary focus of my passion, just as call collecting has become an obsession for others.

Far be it from me to pass up any item with a bit of history and a connection with the turkey. There's the cover from a 1941 magazine featuring Chesterfield cigarettes' "Girl of the Month" carrying a fine gobbler across her shoulder and a shotgun under her arm.

Another treasure is an original pen-and-ink sketch of a solitary gobbler by noted outdoor humorist Ed Zern. Also included are commemorative tokens, state and National Wild Turkey Federation turkey stamps, a sketch of a turkey by the current federal duck stamp contest winner, Adam Grimm, and more. It's all overseen by mounts of two of my finest gobblers and a china cabinet packed with calls. By now, the picture should begin to emerge — this indicates a single-minded pack rat whose study must be a mess.

True enough, and other than the occasional fruitless foray through the room with a vacuum, my long-suffering wife just shakes her head in dismay each time a fellow hunter visits and accepts the study the way it is. What she doesn't fully understand is the common nature of my "lust" — her word, not mine — for the turkey. Across the country, you'll find hundreds of thousands of similarly cluttered dens, basements, garages and studies filled with links to the turkey. I haven't visited their homes, but Brad Harris and Mark Drury confess I would encounter similar scenes of this delightful disarray. Turkey hunting does that to you. It's difficult to pinpoint why.

Sure, the turkey figures prominently in American history. Every school child learns the story of the first Thanksgiving. Sadly, what they often don't learn is that hunting provided the centerpiece of that feast. Most hunters also realize that one of our founding fathers, Benjamin Franklin, had a great affinity for the turkey. Contrary to popular belief, however, he did not propose the bird as our national symbol. Rather, in a letter to his daughter, he unfavorably compared the eagle with the wild turkey after the former had already been chosen as the young nation's symbol.

Tales of hunting and eating turkeys can be found scattered through the diaries and journals of many early American frontier travelers and explorers, although stories of gobblers weighing 50 pounds and similar foolishness can be dismissed. Likewise, you must wonder how much contact the great naturalist John James Audubon had with wild turkeys. His painting of the bird is inferior if not downright inaccurate. For the most part, though, you won't find much attention devoted to turkeys as a sportsman's quarry until well into the 19th century.

The critical explanation likely focuses on market hunting and, probably, the bird's vulnerability. As anyone who has hunted in New Zealand can attest, the turkeys there — until pressured — display almost no wariness. It's possible the same held true of turkeys in Colonial times, although discussions of innate vs. learned behavior regarding interaction with humans are better left to biologists. At any rate, as early as 1848, Frank Forester, in *Field Sports of the United States*, wrote, "This noble and beautiful bird, ... the pride of the forest ... is now all but extinct in the Eastern and Middle States of the Union."

Early hunting methods contributed to the turkey's rapid decline or disappearance through much of its original range. Roost-shooting was common, and most states had no established seasons or limits — daily or annual —

until the beginning of the 20th century. In open areas, turkeys hardly had a chance.

President Theodore Roosevelt wrote about coursing turkeys with greyhounds on the open plains. In fact, this consummate sportsman and conservationist, a founder of the Boone and Crockett Club and a key figure in establishing our nation's system of national parks and forests, failed to see the problems with killing birds on the roost.

The future president's turkey entry in the massive two-volume *Encyclopedia of Sport*, published in 1898, furnishes a capsule of why the turkey came so close to vanishing.

"In the wildest regions," he wrote, "it is still possible to enjoy the fun of shooting turkeys on their roosts." Roosevelt then described this approach. "A goodly number can be shot, especially if those lowest on the branches are selected, before the others will take flight."

Roosevelt's account of hunting turkeys on the plains with greyhounds seems more despicable from today's perspective, because he detailed birds being forced to fly by the fleet dogs until they could no longer take wing.

As troubling as Roosevelt's material might be, it reflects the time and its hunting methods. Should anyone doubt this, read Gen. William E. Strong's *Canadian River Hunt*, which is his journal of a trip with several other military men. What Strong refers to as "rare sport" amounts to a catalog of carnage. He described firing at turkeys until his gun barrel became too hot to touch, crippled birds left to their fate, and of "A Night in the Roost," which could have been entitled "Adventures in a Turkey Abattoir."

Although it's unfair to view yesterday's concept of sport through today's eyes, knowledge of these hunting techniques helps us understand and appreciate modern turkey hunting. During the generation in which Strong was hunting in Oklahoma and Roosevelt was writing about turkeys, the sport was beginning to develop a new, distinctly different face. In regions of the East and South where turkeys had not vanished, they merited the term "wild." Driven into the most remote swamps and deepest hardwoods, they became reclusive and wary. Then, the tactics and techniques we still use to hunt turkeys came into their own.

We know from archaeological evidence that American Indians used wingbone calls long before Europeans arrived. Similarly, pioneer hunters learned how to imitate turkey sounds with their voices or by using the leaves of green briars or other plants. However, references to calling and sport hunting didn't appear much earlier than the last quarter of the 19th century.

Elisha J. Lewis, in his 1854 book *The American Sportsman*, mentioned a friend who told him about calls used in Mississippi. He said that correspondent, Dr. R. Percy Sargent, "Informs us that wild turkeys are still met with, in small numbers, in the cypress swamps, thick forests, and wild ridges ... . They are, of course, very wary, cunning, and watchful of the approach of man, and are only to be killed by those long experienced in hunting them and practically familiar with their habits and secret haunts."

That's the turkey we know today, and although spring hunting has replaced fall hunting as the most popular season, the sport's basic approach and allure remain much like they were more than a century ago.

It was then C.L. Jordan began writing about calls and call making, notably suction-type instruments, in national magazines such as *Forest and Stream* and *Shooting and Fishing*, in the 1880s and 1890s. During that time, the U.S. Patent Office issued patents for various turkey calls, including the famed Gibson-style box.

In 1914, the next generation would see the publication of the first book devoted to turkey hunting: E.A. McIlhenny's *The Wild Turkey and Its Hunting*. The work should actually be credited to C.L. Jordan, who wrote almost all of the book. McIlhenny simply brought it to published fruition after Jordan was killed by a poacher.

Even with the book's appearance and the emergence of famous call makers, such as Tom and Inman Turpin, turkey hunters were an exclusive fraternity for the first half of the 20th century. Although Tom Turpin wrote occasional magazine articles about turkey hunting and Archibald Rutledge penned scores of them, only a handful of other turkey books were written during the era. Turpin did a small book, the original form of which is exceedingly rare — it was reprinted by Penn's Woods in 1966 as *Hunting the Wild Turkey* — and Simon Everitt wrote his delightful 1928 book *Tales of Wild Turkey Hunting*. In 1949, arguably the most important turkey book ever written, Henry Edwards Davis' *The American Wild Turkey*, appeared.

Those pioneering works share a common characteristic: They remind us of the sport's tremendous difficulty. As we have seen, that might not always have been the case. By the 20th century, however, there was no denying the turkey — no matter the subspecies — presented a genuine challenge. Unquestionably, the demands turkeys placed on hunters accounted for much of the sport's allure. A turkey hunter had to be an accomplished woodsman, a capable caller, a hard hunter and gifted with ample patience. The turkey's comeback has done nothing to diminish the bird's appeal or the importance of these traits.

Seemingly, after the magic spark gave turkey hunting its special aura and appeal, it burned with inextinguishable brightness. That continues today, and turkey hunting's lure is at an all-time high — and growing. Although I have subsequently heard many variations of the same analogy, the late Larry Hearn first suggested to me the addictive qualities of turkey hunting. He was a masterful hunter, had meticulously studied the sport, knew intimately the history of call making and wrote one of the most moving tributes to the turkey in *A Turkey Hunter's Prayer*.

"Those government boys think they've got problems with this cocaine- and crack-addiction thing, but they don't know what compulsion and craving are until they meet that hopelessly lost soul known as a turkey hunter," he said with a chuckle.

The hunter has always had affinity for his prey. It might be mentioned infrequently or as an intangible matter, but the hunter's link to the hunted cannot be denied. In the quest for turkeys, however, that linkage seems to expand. Certainly, part of that comes from realizing that we now have — in abundant numbers — a bird we almost lost. It also derives from the turkey's elusiveness and mystique, not to mention its exasperating yet endearing unpredictability.

At this chapter's outset, I mentioned my library of turkey hunting materials. A sampling from some of those works might help capture the essence of what the great American game bird means to those who hunt it.

Charles Whittington's 1971 *Tall Timber Gabriels* likens distant gobbling to the trumpet blower of biblical renown. Bob Saile's 1998 *Sultan of Spring* equates the turkey with royalty. For Horatio Bigelow, a forgotten hunter from yesteryear, the turkey figured prominently in his finding the mother lode he described in 1943 as *Gunnerman's Gold*. In 1991, Jack Dudley, a national calling champion in competitive calling's early days, said the time he spent matching wits with toms was *The Greatest Moments of My Life*, and Earl Groves, one of the NWTF's stalwarts from the outset, offers a play on words with his 1977 *Tomfoolery* and 1997 *Tomfoolery 2000*.

Who can resist Tom Kelly's 1995 *Better on a Rising Tide*, taken from a friend's serious suggestion that he had finally determined, through comparisons with tide tables, why birds gobbled with exceptional vigor some days.

My favorites for capturing the turkey's essence, however, focus on a well-known work and another that's equally obscure. The widely read book was written by the late Gene Nunnery, who had a knack for getting to the heart of the turkey hunting experience. His 1986 *I Will Lift Up Mine Eyes Unto the Hills* — the title was taken from the 23rd Psalm — splendidly relates the turkey's merits to the hunting experience. When Nunnery speaks of the "uncertainty of pursuit," he strikes a chord with the legions who have experienced turkey hunting's vagaries and vicissitudes.

The second work, originally published as an article in 1930, and more recently offered as a small, limited-edition treatise — only 66 copies — with an introduction by Ralf Coykendall, was written by Col. Harold P. Sheldon. In it, he describes the difficulties of turkey hunting.

"It is not an entirely hopeless quest, nor is it necessarily fruitless, even though no turkey is brought to bag," he wrote. "There is a constant skill being put to play which ... is a reward in itself; and there is the charm of variety to urge one along and the hope, never diminishing, that fortune has a gobbler ... waiting for you just at the farther edge of the next clearing."

Those qualities are why Sheldon borrowed the words of an old African-American who had guided him on a hunt and described the turkey as *A Sho-Nuff Noble Bird*.

The turkey is noble and in many senses ennobles those who hunt it.

This book makes no pretense of being of a scientific nature, although it aspires to help you better understand, through the eyes of two experts, the whys and wherefores of successful turkey hunting. Studies of the various subspecies and their biological traits are better left to experts. However, Drury and Harris recommend — and I second this — that you learn more about turkey hunting's scientific side. Good starting points include James C. Dickson's (editor and compiler) 1992 *The Wild Turkey: Biology and Management* or any of Lovett Williams' excellent books.

When Harris and Drury reflect on the turkey, what it has meant to them and how it has shaped their lives, you realize a day dealing with gobblers amounts to more than a few hours afield. It renews and restores the hunter, no matter how many times he does it.

"Once I got started hunting turkeys, it seems I've never been able to get enough of it," Drury said. "If you asked me to explain why, I think it comes down to the nature of the turkey. The sport is so challenging, and the turkey so unpredictable that you have to be intrigued."

Harris remembered his early years as a hunter, and acknowledged that after his grandfather planted a seed through storytelling when he was only 6 or 7, he had to hunt turkeys.

"I picked the brains of anyone who was supposed to know anything about turkeys," he said. "But what held me then and still holds me is the nature of the bird."

So it is for us all: a wary, worthy adversary that returned from the brink of oblivion to brighten our days and lighten our sporting ways.

Section 2
Preparation
Equipment and Education

Calls and Their Use

As instruments of deception and deceit, calls give turkey hunting much of its aura. They let hunters interact with the hunted in a manner and to a degree seldom otherwise encountered. In fact, only elk hunting provides comparable interchange, and even then, the vocabulary is somewhat limited. As we'll see in Chapter 8, woodsmanship looms larger than calling for killing turkeys, but the heart of the sport's excitement is communicating with a gobbler.

The fact you can talk to an edgy creature — one that gives new meaning to wildness — is exhilarating. When a series of soft yelps, so perfectly produced they seem to belong to nature, brings an instant, nearby response, the thrill is almost indescribable.

The rattling of a gobble seems like a cross between an earthquake and a cannon explosion. At close range, it can turn a typically calm, stable person into a quivering mass of protoplasm. The knee supporting your gun suddenly seems to dance and come to life. You become vaguely aware of your racing pulse, and no matter the temperature, a cold sweat seems to soak you. Suddenly, panic wants to become your best friend.

Those who haven't lived the experience heap ridicule on turkey hunters, saying it's ludicrous that a 20-pound bird could evoke such emotions. Yet the moments after a thunderous gobble are some of the most tension-laden, nerve-wracking ones in history. Although they wring you dry and leave you emotionally exhausted, they are the moments we seek.

The anticipation is delicious. Reversing nature's course and piquing a gobbler's curiosity so he comes to you — when the hen is supposed to go to him — is a high accomplishment. Then, at the moment of truth, as you squeeze your gun's trigger, you are sated with rare satisfaction. You have met nature on her terms and triumphed.

The aftermath is anticlimactic. In fact, as you stand over a black-and-bronze monarch, with sun slanting and shimmering off its feathers in a kaleidoscope of colors, bittersweetness sets in. One of nature's most splendid creatures lies dead, and the magnitude of that splendor requires respect — even reverence. To realize that you called the bird within range is to be struck with awe, and no matter how many times it happens, your sense of wonder remains.

Archibald Rutledge, one of my favorite writers, had a knack with titles. Who can resist "Fireworks in the Peafield Corner" or "The Bishop Earns a Gobbler?" For a tempting title, though, my favorite is "Miss Seduction Struts Her Stuff." Miss Seduction was a box call Rutledge crafted, and he later made others he advertised in *Field & Stream* for $5 (they bring almost $1,000 today on the collectibles market). Never mind that the calls were poorly made and sounded more like a sore-tailed cat than a sweet hen.

The name Miss Seduction is inspired, and the play on the word strut, as applied to turkeys, is pure genius. Countless similarly expressive monikers have been given to turkey calls. In fact, a quick peek at a packed display cabinet feet from where I write this provides many examples. From Lohman Calls, with which Brad Harris has been associated for many years, I have the Double Thunder box call, the Thunder Dome series of friction calls and the Hot Single, a diaphragm Harris designed. From Mark Drury's M.A.D. Calls, I have the Hammer and Double Barrel box call. Other examples include Sweet Lips, Old Irresistible, the Spirit Yelper, Sweet Thing, the Enticer and the Tantalizer.

Names alone mean little, but there's no doubt about the intent. They are tools of allure; instruments designed to tempt and enchant. When it comes to calling a turkey, Drury and Harris are acknowledged masters. They are talented hunters who elicit turkey sounds from calls the way a virtuoso violinist brings sweet sounds from his instrument's strings. They can do so partly because of exceptional ability. However, their ear for the turkey's music —and it is music to a hunter — would mean little if they hadn't paid their dues through incredible amounts of time afield. They learned not on the contest stage, but in the ultimate theater of competition — an arena where the judges sleep in trees rather than sit in chairs. What follows is a detailed calling session with two of the finest.

The first thing Drury mentioned could almost be described as his trademark — high pitch.

"I've always focused on high-pitched calls no matter what the type," he said. "I have studied the voice of the turkey extensively using spectrograms, and my research revealed that excited turkeys talk at a high pitch, just like humans do when they are excited."

While gathering materials for this book, I dug through my old files and found how meticulous Drury has been during the evolution of high-frequency calling. My reference material contained test results that compared gobbling response with call frequency. Drury used three calls that had been analyzed by a spectrogram to determine their frequency. One peaked at 5,000 hertz, the second at 10,000 hertz and the third at 15,000 hertz. Of 279 birds hunters saw and called to, 93 responded. No turkey gobbled only to the 5,000-hertz call, and only one gobbled solely to the 10,000-hertz model. However, 78 of the 93 responsive birds gobbled to the 15,000-hertz call, and of those, 35 responded only to the high-frequency call.

That might be more data than most readers want, but the numbers reveal proof in the high-frequency pudding. With such background, Drury's devotion to high pitch becomes understandable.

Harris also believes in high-frequency calls and uses them regularly. Interestingly, he and Drury combined to develop one of the most noteworthy call breakthroughs in recent decades: a call that produces low sounds that are anything but penetrating. The Spit-n-Drum, an adjustable or tunable bellows-type call, imitates the spitting-like sound followed by the low hum a gobbler makes when it struts.

Harris had tinkered with the idea for some time, and when he neared the answer, he shared his findings with Drury. The pair fine-tuned the call so it was ready to be marketed. The final product produced a sound that was nonvocal yet intimately associated with breeding. Because it can stimulate a gobbler's curiosity, and touch a tom's sense of dominance and territoriality, the call adds an important, different weapon to a hunter's arsenal.

If Drury's trademark is high pitch, Harris' is aggressiveness. Anyone who has watched and analyzed his calling will realize that.

"I've found that aggressive, confident calling works best for me," he said. "That runs contrary to the wisdom that was standard among old-timers, and I won't deny that you can kill turkeys taking a much more conservative approach. For me, though, after I had sufficient confidence in my calling and

WHEN IT COMES TO CALLING TECHNIQUES, Harris likes "to make things happen." Aggressive calling is part of that, but he also switches calls and varies how he yelps or cutts. What works one day might not work the next, so you have to keep testing the waters until you hit the right sound.

had developed a sense of how to read a turkey's temperature, my calling usually followed an approach where I really took it to the gobbler.

"Obviously, you have to factor in other things. Unquestionably, there are times when you need to tone things down and keep your calling subdued."

Like Drury, Harris wants to produce excitement in turkeys, and he generates that through aggressive calling.

"There are enough turkeys today that you can afford to take some chances with calling," he said. "I'm convinced that in the final analysis, you will get more birds to the gun by being aggressive in your calling."

Also, Harris said, that approach isn't limited to highly experienced hunters.

"If you practice with your calls and develop your calling skills to the point where you can yelp, cluck, purr and make the other common calls consistently, you should be confident," he said. "Also, remember that you don't have to sound like a contest caller. Real turkeys sometimes sound awful, and if you hit a bad note or make a poor call, just keep going."

An error followed by sudden silence is most likely to alert a gobbler that something isn't kosher.

Harris also suggested you pay special attention to rhythm.

"I believe the timing or the cadence of the call is more important than getting the sound exactly right every time," he said. "If you listen to hens yelp, you'll notice they make all sorts of sounds. But the timing they're delivered with is consistent, and callers need to strive for that same consistency."

Drury also favors aggressive calling.

"I like active — not passive — turkey hunting," he said. "My calling reflects my personality."

Both hunters believe in versatility. Their vests contain an impressive variety of calls, and they likely use most of them during a day afield. From my observations, you can count on boxes, slates and diaphragms appearing repeatedly during a day.

In addition, Drury and Harris try different versions of each type of call and vary the way they use a specific call.

From watching them hunt and paying attention to the calls they use, diaphragm calls come first for Drury and Harris.

"I like a two-reed diaphragm," Drury said. However, he quickly added that the Super Aluminator, a friction call he developed, "has figured in more turkeys I've killed or called in for others to shoot than any single call."

Because the Aluminator resulted from Drury's work with high-frequency, that seems appropriate.

When it comes to calling techniques, Harris likes "to make things happen." Aggressive calling is part of that, but he also uses another tactic.

"Another way is through experimentation," he said. "When trying to locate birds, for example, I frequently switch calls and vary the manner in which I yelp or cutt. What works one day might not work the next, and you have to keep testing the waters until you hit the right sound."

For stimulating a gobbler's interest, Drury believes in switching sounds.

"The gobbler might think there's more than one hen there, or it might just be that something new provides extra stimulation," he said. "But when calling, I make it a point to change sounds. You can do this through changing calls or by running one call in a different way. I change calls most often when trying to locate a bird, but if a gobbler I'm working seems to lose interest, then it's time to try something different.

"The measure of a good turkey hunter is someone who can read birds and their moods. He then adjusts his calling accordingly."

Harris' evaluation of the connection between calling and success echoes Drury's.

"The ability to call well comes in large part from studying and understanding turkeys," he said. "A good turkey hunter can figure out what a gobbler wants and then give him that kind of calling."

Through the years, Harris and Drury have developed a knack for knowing gobblers' whims and recognizing the type of calling a situation requires.

"There's always some trial and error involved, and it's better to make mistakes and learn from them than to get in a rut and remain in it," he said. "You learn by trying various calling techniques, and if you never experiment, how can you know whether something will work?"

Drury said one of the most common mistakes hunters make is to do the same thing repeatedly.

"It's almost as if the hunter looks at his watch and says to himself, 'Every 10 minutes, I need to yelp five times,'" he said. "Don't make the mistake of getting into a repetitive pattern. The old saying about variety being the spice of life applies to calling."

That is, you never know what will work until you try it. When you go afield, work to refine and diversify your calling techniques.

THE PROS AND CONS OF VARIOUS CALLS

As we've seen, Harris and Drury are experts with various calls. Similarly, you should strive to develop good calling skills with at least three types of calls. It's fine to have a favorite — that reliable model you consider your No. 1 call — and use it most of the time. When it fails, though, you must have several aces in the hole. You should be able to produce common turkey sounds — notably hen yelps, clucks, cutts and purrs — on several calls. Even after you master several calls, experiment and tinker, like the Outland experts.

➤ Box calls are probably the easiest call to learn, and they can produce most turkey sounds. In addition to hen sounds, a box with a clapper lid can also render reasonable gobbles when circled with a rubber band that has the correct tension.

Boxes have several weaknesses. You cannot kee-kee on them, and must use two hands and quite a bit of movement to operate them. In addition, boxes become useless when wet. They can also be cumbersome, require constant chalking to sound their best, and almost invite breakage if you fall or sit carelessly. Innovations, such as push-button boxes and making boxes from materials other than wood, have addressed some of those problems.

➤ Diaphragms are the most widely used turkey call. They come in many variations, including single reeds to stacks of up to four reeds, and feature various types of slits, cuts and reed arrangements.

Diaphragms require almost no movement and can reproduce all the sounds in a turkey's vocabulary. Weather doesn't affect diaphragms, although you shouldn't leave them on the dash of your truck or where they can dry out.

Some people tend to choke when they use mouth calls. Also, diaphragms are so popular that turkeys can become accustomed to them. Other problems include a lack of volume for long-range calling, a relatively short life span as latex wears out, and a certain lack of sound sweetness compared to a slate or wingbone call.

➤ Friction calls are often called slates, but that's misleading because friction calls are now constructed from many materials, including glass, ceramic, aluminum, titanium and crystal.

One of a friction call's greatest assets — this is especially true with true slates — is the ability to produce exact turkey sounds. Most competitive callers and experienced hunters believe slates sound more like real turkeys

DRURY CLAIMS THE SUPER ALUMINATOR, a friction call he developed, "has figured in more turkeys I've killed or called in for others to shoot than any single call." Here, Drury holds the Aluminator for maximum carry while trying to get a shock gobble.

than any other call. Friction calls are also excellent for soft calling, such as purrs and muted clucks.

Moisture can be a problem, although some new friction calls include strikers that let them operate when wet. However, if the pot holding the call is made of wood — and wood produces fine sounds — rain or dampness can still deter the sound.

Also, the sound from many friction calls doesn't carry well, although others, such as the Aluminator, scream when you bear down on them.

➤ Tube calls are used much less than boxes, diaphragms and friction calls, but they're great for locating turkeys. Their sound carries well, and they can produce realistic gobbles.

Tubes can be difficult to use, and you must replace the latex somewhat frequently. Some hunters find that running air across the tube's latex reed produces an uncomfortable tickling sensation.

➤ Wingbones and trumpet yelpers are probably the least-used calls, mostly because they're difficult to master. Wingbones, especially when heard at some distance, offer exceptionally realistic turkey sounds. They can produce most hen sounds, except purring. Wingbones are especially good for locating birds, and turkeys seem to gobble at them when they ignore other calls.

Although wingbones aren't affected by weather, they are fragile and require two hands to operate.

True wingbone calls, those made from the wingbones of wild turkeys, are unavailable on the mass market.

Locator Calls and Their Use

Few aspects of turkey hunting generate more excitement than hearing a gobble. At times, turkeys seem to gobble at anything, but other times — maybe the next hour or next day — they seem to have lockjaw. Therein lies the challenge, because you must find a gobbler before you can hunt him.

Occasionally, you can locate birds by seeing them, usually with binoculars. Typically, however, the locating game involves sound. That's why locator calls figure so significantly in turkey hunting. If you can get a turkey to gobble, you know about where he is. You might not be able to course him precisely, but at least your spirits will be lifted, and you can set up and call knowing the tom hears you.

Brad Harris explained the matter in a way every hunter can appreciate.

"If you can find them, there's a chance to work them," he said. "Otherwise, you wonder if you are whistling in the wind, so to speak. But after you know a gobbler is there, you're excited and give the hunt your best."

The confidence and concentration that come from locating a bird are important. Locator calls help you find toms, but they also help you other ways. After you have pinpointed a bird and switch to turkey talk, a gobbler knows exactly where you are after your first clucks or yelps. For example, he knows you are at the base of that big white oak 10 feet from the old logging road where he likes to strut. You are in his living room. Not even modern technology can rival his built-in Global Positioning System, and he never has to replace batteries. After that gobbler hears yelping or other turkey sounds, he has you located and can find you if he wants to.

That incredible internal compass can pose problems, and that's another reason for using locator calls. They let you move into position — or reposition when a tom proves uncooperative — without worrying about a gobbler coming to investigate your turkey calling. If you can get a bird to gobble at a locator call, you know where he is and feel secure about making cautious moves.

When you yelp, although it might be equally productive for provoking a gobbler, you run the risk that he might make his move. If he moves while you are moving, the result is the same every time — a boogered bird.

Drury and Harris believe locator calling deserves more study, practice and application than most hunters give it. They use locator calls extensively, have studied what it takes to trip a tom's vocal switch and are convinced their locating abilities make them more successful. After all, locating a gobbler is the critical first step to a successful hunt.

Many sounds can make a turkey gobble. I have kept a list of sounds — slightly fewer than 100 — that have evoked responses from longbeards. Of course, I've heard predictable ones, such as owls hooting, crows cawing and hawks screaming. However, I've also heard turkeys gobble at a youngster screaming while playing, a bulldozer's warning signal from a distant dump, airplanes backing off while in holding patterns, and a railroad repair-crew worker yelling to a buddy. In fact, a good friend and fellow writer uses his voice to produce something that sounds like a cross between a dying woman and a cat with its tail caught in a meat grinder. It's an awful racket that has no place in nature — or even what poses as music among today's adolescents — but it makes turkeys gobble.

Turkeys might gobble at any time, but locator calls unquestionably work best at and just before daylight. They can also work well at roosting time, when they help you find a longbeard to hunt the next morning. However, in certain situations, Harris and Drury use several types of locating methods throughout the day, including locator calls, their voices and, occasionally, turkey calls.

The logical place to begin a detailed examination of locating is with that magical time, which can last a half hour to 90 minutes on overcast days, when birds have awakened but have not left the roost. Gobblers — dominant and subordinate birds — seem determined to greet the dawn with gobbles. After they are on the ground, many subordinate gobblers — which are farther down the pecking order and have suffered drubbings at the onset of mating season — dare not utter a sound. On the roost, however, they seem secure and are willing to gobble. In areas where turkeys are plentiful, the result can be a crescendo of gobbling. With the possible exception of traditional roosts along some Texas rivers, nowhere is this more apparent than Drury and Harris' Midwestern stomping grounds. On clear, calm and crisp late-April Missouri mornings, I have heard gobbles roll toward me from the east like dominoes of sound tumbling upon another as they play nature's keyboard.

Many spring veterans prefer to let "nature do the locating" when possible. That is, they wait to see if any common daylight sounds — crows feuding, or a barred owl's distinctive, haunting eight-note call — evoke a gobble. Only when this fails will they call.

The two most commonly used locators — owl hooters and crow calls — are associated with dawn. Like turkeys, owls and crows tend to be vocal at dawn. Owls, which are nocturnal, usually become quiet after daylight arrives, although it's not unusual for one to tune up in late afternoon. Sometimes, this leads to the eerie laughing or cackling sounds of several owls conversing, and that can get turkeys gobbling at what ordinarily is one of their least vocal periods. Highly talkative, crows can break out in garrulous conversation almost any time. Often, intense, prolonged crow calling occurs when they chase hawks or owls. Also, they "devil" turkeys by repeatedly dive-bombing them and fussing. Therefore, a crow call can locate turkeys any time, and it's probably the most versatile, widely used locator.

Several other birds commonly tune up at dawn, and those that make loud, penetrating noises cause the most gobbling. Canada geese and great blue herons are particularly noteworthy. Similarly, the keen squeals of wood ducks can also provoke reactions from nearby turkeys.

As day progresses, other bird sounds enter the picture. There's the staccato cry of the pileated woodpecker, which is so sudden and startling that folks in the Carolina Low Country often refer to them as Lord God Birds ("Lord God, what made that noise?"). Hawks screaming during mating rituals or in anger also get attention, as does the cry of a peacock. Commercial calls can imitate these sounds, and most hunters carry several in their vests.

Then there's what many hunters swear is the finest locator call: a coyote howler. The adaptable coyote has expanded its range so much it can be found anywhere in turkey country, so this should be no surprise. Of course, logic might hold that turkeys should shut up immediately when they hear coyotes yipping, whining or howling, because coyotes sometimes feast on turkeys. That's not the case. Many shock-gobbles likely result from the suddenness and loudness of a sound, not association with a specific animal.

65

When I hunted New Zealand, turkeys gobbled like crazy at my rather inept natural-voice owling, although New Zealand has no barred owls. We'll likely never know just what makes a longbeard shock-gobble, but the word shock is unquestionably critical.

"It's loud, sudden sounds that make turkeys gobble," Drury said.

That has guided most of his efforts in designing and using locators.

"I have consistently made a practice of listening in the woods and making mental notes of what makes turkeys gobble," Drury said. "I want my locator calls to have the same sort of impact as those sounds."

A good example is a new coyote howler that should become available about the time this book appears. It will have two versions, including a custom cherry-wood call that should appeal to collectors and hunters.

"We are also producing crow and owl calls in the custom version," Drury said. "Before long, I expect locators to have much of the collectible appeal we have seen associated with turkey calls in recent years.

"To me, there's little doubt about what makes the coyote howler so effective. It consistently hits 15,000 to 16,000 hertz every time, and it's so piercing and penetrating that the ears of anyone standing nearby actually hurt when the howler is used."

Having heard a prototype during a Spring 2000 Colorado hunt, I can attest to that. It only took one blast for me. Afterward, when I listened for a gobbler, I was many yards away from Drury.

Although he's especially fond of the coyote howler, Drury said it's critical to know when to use various calls. Also, he's convinced hunters should constantly switch sounds.

"If a hunter walks through the woods at daylight constantly crow calling or owling, the shock value soon vanishes, along with loudness," he said. "It's novelty that gets results. If I could offer one tip on locator calls, it would be to switch sounds. The same thing that holds true for using turkey calls — the virtues of versatility — also applies to locators."

As you've learned, some of Harris' earliest success in competitive calling came from his owl-hooting abilities. In the late 1970s, he used his natural voice when few others did, although that approach has become common in contests and the woods.

"Maybe as good an indication of my views on the importance of locating is provided by the first cassette I did," he said. "It was entitled *Owl Hooting and Turkey Locating*, and the information it provided more than two decades

Brad Harris

SOME OF HARRIS' EARLIEST SUCCESS in competitive calling came from his owl-hooting abilities. In the late 1970s, he used his natural voice when few others did, although that approach has become common in contests and the woods.

ago holds true.

"While working on the tape, some thoughts I had already developed in my early hunting experiences were reinforced. Foremost among these was realizing that finding turkeys by using locator calls in the pre-season was something smart hunters should be able to do reasonably well. I also realized locators could work well throughout the day. That might seem pretty standard now, but it wasn't in the 1970s. Some old-timers knew that, I'm sure, but the knowledge wasn't general by any means. It belongs to the modern era of turkey hunting."

Harris also learned about the importance of variety.

"After I mastered a crow call, I had made a quantum leap, and not just because I could owl and caw well," he said. "That ability led me to develop my capabilities with other locators. For me, the next step was getting the sound of a woodpecker down pat."

Harris has learned the effectiveness of locators varies with weather and time of day.

"I love to use a pileated woodpecker call on still, bluebird days," he said.

"Somehow, turkeys seem to respond to it when they ignore most everything else. When it comes to hawk calls, screams are most effective for me in the late morning and early afternoon, and they work best when a turkey is close. Hawk calling just doesn't bring gobbles from great distances the way a coyote howl or even owling will do.

"Speaking of coyotes, my first hunt in Texas was a real revelation. I tried owling, and the Rio Grandes paid little attention. That might not have worked, but the howls and barking yips of a coyote were like magic. The first thing I did after that experience was to go back and begin working on an open-reed howler."

The result was Lohman's Model 281 Coyote Howler.

"I still use it religiously, even today," he said. "It's great for roosting birds at dusk in conditions with high winds and bad weather."

Just as Drury stressed the effectiveness of specific, calculated approaches, Harris said hunters need a game plan for finding gobblers.

"I think it is best to sound natural," he said, adding that he believes in high volume and pitch. Still, you never know what will happen on a given day. Sometimes, turkeys answer the first sound, but others need teasing or tweaking. But get it in your mind that you need to be willing to experiment and take their temperature until you find what the birds want."

Harris said hunters should start simple.

"There's no set rule, except you must give them what they want," he said. "I have no question that turkeys lock in on a specific sound and respond accordingly, with locators and regular calls. The only problem is that in each instance, that varies from day to day."

LOCATING WITH TURKEY SOUNDS

As most hunters realize — and we'll cover this in "Safety and Ethics" — using turkey sounds to locate birds holds some inherent dangers. These mostly occur when a tom decides it wants to be where calling is coming from — in a hurry. You can get busted when a gobbler runs a 400-meter dash to the seductive hen and you aren't ready. However, when properly used, turkey sounds — gobbling and hen calling — can be great locators.

"You shouldn't forget that yelping can produce shock-gobbles just like crowing or owling," Drury said.

Drury's work with high-frequency sound has led him to believe a sudden series of yelps — especially when the pitch is extremely high — works well

WHEN PROPERLY USED, turkey sounds — gobbling and hen calling — can be great locators. "You shouldn't forget that yelping can produce shock-gobbles just like crowing or owling," Drury said.

TYPICALLY, THE LOCATING GAME involves sound. That's why locator calls figure so significantly in turkey hunting. If you can get a turkey to gobble, you know about where he is. Here, Mark Drury calls and Don Shipp listens.

when trying to strike birds.

"I noticed years ago that certain types of calls that carried well and were high pitched — wingbones, boat paddles and tube calls — seemed to perform especially well for getting longbeards to respond," he said.

From that, he worked to develop aluminum and titanium friction calls. Even recent M.A.D. box calls can produce high pitch.

Most long-distance locating with turkey calls involves yelping, at least partly because high-pitched yelps carry well. However, frenzied lost calls occasionally produce gobbles, and aggressive cutting can trip a tom's switch. Various hen sounds belong in your locating repertoire because they form essential parts of your turkey-working technique.

Gobbler sounds can also locate turkeys. Harris said you can use spring gobblers' combative, territorial instincts to your advantage for finding birds. Gobbling, whether with a shaker, diaphragm or voice, can rouse a tom.

"Obviously, you need to think carefully before you gobble," Harris said. "Safety figures here, and in my opinion, no one should resort to gobbling on public land. Also, gobbling can have a negative impact on subordinate or satellite birds. They might leave the area rather than risk an encounter with what presumably is a dominant bird."

Still, when nothing else works, and where it can be done safely, gobbling deserves an occasional try.

It really doesn't matter whether you use locator calls, offbeat sounds or turkey sounds.

"What does matter," Drury said, "is that a well-rounded hunter has significant skills for finding birds. He knows what works for him, and no one can deny the significance of being able to make birds gobble. It adds to the appeal of the experience, and anyone who doesn't thrill to the sound of a gobble probably should find something else. Also, you can't argue with the fact that it's easier to hunt turkeys if you hear them and know they are there."

Harris summed things up when he said, "Most turkey hunters underuse locators."

That contains a simple, straightforward message. Work on your calling skills, but remember they involve more than imitating a turkey. The competent use of locators is something for which every hunter should strive. Sometimes, that skill can make the difference.

Guns and Loads

One of the best indications of how far turkey hunting has progressed is that dozens of guns — not to mention chokes and shotshells — have been developed for the sport.

Peruse hunting magazines of yesteryear. You will be fascinated by the stories and ads, not to mention astounded by the increase of gun prices. Search as much as you like, though, for a turkey gun. You won't find one. Other than an occasional story and a rare ad for calls, you might assume turkey hunting didn't exist. Of course, in many places, it didn't.

That's part of the past, though, and we're dealing with current tools that let hunters close the deal. For now, let's focus on guns and shotshells.

The choice of each depends largely on individual hunters. A small youngster or woman, for example, has no business carrying a 10-gauge — and probably not a 12-gauge. Similarly, a hunter who insists on taking 45- to 50-yard shots should avoid No. 7½ shot like the whooping cough. For folks who like to see the gleam in a turkey's eye before they pull the trigger, those No. 7½ high-brass shells might be best.

I killed my first turkey with a little Stevens Model 220A 20-gauge. Choked a tight full and chambered to handle 2¾- or 3-inch shells, it handled No. 5 and 6 shot like a dream. The reason I carried it, however, had nothing to do with performance and everything to do with nostalgia. That was my first shotgun as a boy, a Christmas present for my 10th birthday, which my father told me years later had cost him a whopping $29.95. The gun had seen me through boyhood adventures for rabbits and squirrels, and although it was anything but ideal for wing-shooting, it had killed many grouse and bobwhites. At 30 yards, it remains a deadly turkey gun, and there's a message there.

73

What that suggests, simply, is that you don't have to buy a so-called turkey gun to be a turkey hunter. With some contemplation, plenty of patterning and understanding of a gun's capabilities, whatever shotgun you own should be satisfactory. However, there's more than a little truth in spousal comments about "grown boys and their toys," and most serious turkey hunters eventually want a gun designed for one purpose. The nature of that gun and the loads it uses provide endless debate among turkey hunters, and the Outland experts acknowledge there's ample room for choice. As you will see, they have distinctly different preferences for guns and loads. However, everyone seeks some common attributes in a turkey gun, and we'll also consider these. Let's examine the basic types of guns used by turkey hunters, evaluating their strengths and shortcomings.

PART 1: GUNS
TYPES OF GUNS

➤ Pumps. These tough, reliable, easily operated and relatively inexpensive shotguns have long been the choice of budget-conscious hunters or folks who want a gun that does it all. That old standby, the Remington Model 870, provides a good example. In the modern era, several pump shotguns, such as Winchester's Model 1300, have been designed specifically for turkey hunting.

Price and the ability to take a licking and keep on kicking — a hard-hunting turkey enthusiast will likely be rough on a gun — are solid arguments for a pump. Most of the pump-gun's potential problems come from operator error, including short-stroking when pumping to chamber another shell. Although you'll seldom notice recoil while hunting, it comes into play when patterning, and lightweight pumps shooting magnum turkey loads can deliver a shoulder-bruising wallop.

As with any single-barreled gun, a pump doesn't provide any choice when it comes to the choke. You're stuck with whatever tube you screw in, whether the turkey is a few feet or 40 yards away. The only adjustment you can make is to use a second shotshell with a larger shot size.

➤ Semiautomatics. Most modern special-purpose turkey guns are gas-operated semiautomatics. They absorb plenty of recoil, and provide an immediate followup shot. That might seem minor because most turkeys are killed with only one shot. However, once or twice, I've shamefully missed a turkey only to have the bird extend its neck a bit more, straining to see what produced that sudden noise.

74

Brad Harris

MOST SERIOUS TURKEY HUNTERS eventually want a gun designed for one purpose. Brad Harris said a shotgun's characteristics might not be the most important consideration. He believes you must have faith in your gun above all else.

Had it been necessary to shuck a hull out with a pump, the birds would likely have flown immediately. Once, I was shooting a semiautomatic, and the other time I was using a double-barrel, which meant I just had to aim better and squeeze the second trigger.

The biggest objection to semiautomatics, other than their single choke, is that this type of gun is notoriously finicky, sometimes suffering from stuck shells, lockups and the like. Most foul-ups occur when the action is clogged with grit or dust. However, knowing the cause offers no consolation when you watch a gobbler walk away while you vainly struggle to clear a hull or determine why the gun won't fire.

➤ Single-shot shotguns. Really, two categories of shotguns offer single-shot actions, because muzzleloaders and modern single-shots fit this description.

Black-powder weapons really fall into their own realm, however, because few hunters use them as their primary turkey guns. There might come a time when muzzleloaders, as with deer hunters in many states, have a season — perhaps a week — of their own. If this glad day arrives, you can find several guns that will do the trick. Black-powder genius Tony Knight of Modern Muzzleloading has already produced a muzzle-loading shotgun that patterns comparably to the best-shooting modern shotguns. Until we have separate muzzleloading seasons for turkeys, however, black-powder guns belong to folks seeking the highest challenge.

As for modern single-shots, whether with hammers or hammerless, their major virtues include low cost and simplicity of function. They also make inexpensive first turkey guns for youngsters or women, perhaps in 20-gauge rather than 12-gauge.

Single-shots are easily mastered. Basically, all you must do is break down the gun, insert a shell, and know how to cock the hammer or push off the safety.

The primary negative is obvious. You only get one shot, because a turkey won't likely hang around to watch you open the gun, eject the shell, insert another and close the gun. That would rank alongside of a golfer making consecutive holes-in-one.

Some single-shot guns, especially lighter ones, kick like a wall-eyed mule. Of course, that can be alleviated considerably by a shock-absorbing butt plate or by using a heavier gun.

➤ Double-barrels and over-and-unders. Stack-barrels or side-by-sides receive relatively little use from the turkey hunting fraternity. However, look for more turkey-specific double-barrels to emerge in the near future.

Their major advantage, which is highly significant, provides hunters with options when it's time to shoot. A choke that produces a tight pattern at 40 yards functions almost like a rifle at 20. With a second choke, however, say a modified along with an extra-full, you can — with just a push of the barrel selector or choice of a trigger — adjust. That's a welcome characteristic, and it also lets you have different loads in each barrel. You might want No. 4 shot in the barrel with the tighter choke and No. 6 or 7½ shot in the other.

Further, double-barrels and over-and-unders afford reliable performance. You don't have to worry about recycling, hung-up shells or the like.

The biggest problems with two-barreled guns is cost — they are appreciably more expensive than pumps or semiautos — and the fact that few turkey-specific models have been developed. Look for that to change, with camouflage and screw-in turkey chokes soon becoming more prevalent in double-barrels.

GUN CHARACTERISTICS

➤ Camouflage. Although camouflage might not be a must on a turkey gun, you don't want your gun to have shiny spots, which could let a sharp-eyed gobbler spot you.

Older approaches to camouflage, such as tape or fitted sleeves, might be messy or unattractive, but the dipping process, which has almost become standard with turkey guns, lacks nothing in aesthetic appeal.

➤ Swivels and slings. Most turkey guns come with swivels and a sling, as they should. You need a sling for the long treks and hard climbing the sport involves, not to mention keeping your hands free. If a factory sling doesn't suit you, it's easy to upgrade.

Swivels should be quiet and designed so the sling can easily be removed. Many hunters like to take off their slings when they set up, fearing it could get in the way or swing noticeably when they move or mount the gun.

➤ Butt plates. A butt plate capable of absorbing considerable recoil belongs on every turkey gun. The loads needed to kill a gobbler are too powerful for a thin plate to suffice. This might require — especially with guns not manufactured for turkey hunting — installing a new butt plate.

You'll find plenty of plates available.

"Fit is the key," Harris said.

ALTHOUGH CAMOUFLAGE MIGHT NOT be a must on a turkey gun, you don't want your gun to have shiny spots, which could let a sharp-eyed gobbler spot you.

➤ Sights. Although a single sight or bead is standard on most shotguns, turkey guns usually feature two beads or, increasingly, some type of illuminated sights.

"I don't like illuminated sights, and I don't use them on my bow, either," Harris said.

However, many folks do. Illuminated sights can be especially valuable in low light and for folks who have trouble getting their cheeks down on the stock.

➤ Scopes. Various scopes are available to turkey hunters. Models that use a red-dot system or determine when a turkey is in range are especially popular.

Scopes can minimize the likelihood of a miss, but they have several potential liabilities, including being jarred loose, fogging up during damp or rainy conditions, problems with batteries going dead on red-dot systems, and making it difficult to get on a turkey that has begun walking away.

➤ Safeties. As we'll see, Drury and Harris have specific thoughts about safeties.

Quietness and ease of use are essential, and any gun with a safety that's loud or difficult to move presents problems. Location, to some degree, is a matter of preference, but a thumb safety requires slightly less movement and is more visible.

Although these basic features are important when choosing a turkey gun, Harris said a shotgun's characteristics might not be the most important consideration. He believes you must have faith in your gun above all else.

"I've experimented with guns a great deal," he said, "and out of that I've learned some valuable lessons. Among them, confidence comes first. I had a season back in 1976 or 1977 when I missed 13 gobblers."

Harris considers that his best and worst of times as a turkey hunter.

"I worked a lot of birds and got them in close only to miss again and again," he said. "I traded guns, changed loads, patterned repeatedly, and then headed to the woods to miss another one. In a period of less than two weeks, I went through five or six guns. Finally, I realized my misery had nothing to do with the gun. Instead, I had gotten so disconsolate and down that I literally was thinking myself into missing. My confidence level was zero."

Harris eventually turned things around with, as Hank Williams Jr. describes it, an attitude adjustment. He cleared his mind, began to think positively and resumed his role as an effective, successful turkey hunter.

"That was a terrible ordeal," he said, "but as I've said, in one sense it was the best of times. That was because I learned a lesson I'll never forget, and it's one I'm happy to share with every turkey hunter."

Harris believes there's no single sure-fire solution to the gun-and-load equation. However, he has firm thoughts about what you should do.

"Get a gun that fits, is comfortable, patterns well and that you like," he said. "If it functions well and you have confidence in it, you've got your turkey gun."

What's Harris' current turkey gun?

"I've tried everything from a 10-gauge goose gun with a 36-inch barrel to high dollar semiautomatics," he said. "After many years and a lot of guns, I've narrowed things down to where I have a clear idea of what suits me. I want a 12-gauge gun that shoots 3-inch shells and offers multiple shots. I'm comfortable with a pump or semiautomatic, but I prefer the gun be fairly light. I'll sacrifice extra recoil to save a pound or two, because when you carry a gun all day, that weight can make a real difference."

Harris prefers a barrel no longer than 26 inches so he can "get through the woods without the gun catching a lot of limbs."

When it comes to shooting, Harris emphasizes a gun's pattern.

"I want at least 85 percent of the pellets to go in a 30-inch circle at 40 yards," he said, "but I don't worry about extraordinary density of more than 90 percent. As long as you have no holes in the pattern, that's what matters."

Harris has also tried many types of sights.

"For me, what works best is a ventilated rib and double beads, and I prefer contrasting colors on the two beads," he said. "That's fairly simple, and for the most part, I'm a believer in keeping things simple when it comes to a turkey gun."

His thoughts on gun camouflage confirm that.

"Wrapping or a sleeve — anything to get rid of the shine — works just fine," Harris said, "but you can't beat today's dipped guns."

Harris' specific gun choices indicate he's serious about his no-frills, keep-it-simple approach.

"The two models I've used most — and with the most success — through the years say a lot about my outlook," he said. "I've killed a lot of turkeys with a Remington 1100 using the factory choke that came with it, and I have a Mossberg 835 that has served me well. I did have to have the safety reworked on it (it was too stiff, a frequent problem with Mossberg's early 835s), but I like its location. To me, a top or thumb safety is convenient because I can see it."

Drury's experience with turkey guns has followed the precise scientific path that typifies much of his career. Not surprisingly, he differs from Harris on several gun preferences.

"Developing the M.A.D. Max choke led me to do lots of experimentation," he said. "I wanted to get all of the shotshell's pellets in and out of the choke tube together, and with 2 ounces of No. 6 shot, it turned out that a .655-constriction choke did the trick. I learned that only after considerable study and thought, along with picking Mark Banser's brain (Banser is considered a gunsmithing guru who specializes in turkey guns) on forcing cones, patterns and related matters. The result was a choke with the industry's longest porting system. It throws a tight, efficient pattern of 96 percent to 97 percent in a 30-inch circle at 40 yards."

While working on M.A.D. Max, Drury fired hundreds of rounds of various shotshells from the three leading ammunition manufacturers — Federal,

"MY RECOMMENDATION IS TO FIND the combination of shotshell and after-market choke that works best in your gun," Brad Harris said. "That sometimes takes some work and expense, but in the end, you'll have a gun that fits your needs and with which you are confident and comfortable."

Remington and Winchester — along with some other companies' special turkey shells.

"My recommendation is to find the combination of shotshell and after-market choke that works best in your gun," he said. "That sometimes takes some work and expense, but in the end, you'll have a gun that fits your needs and with which you are confident and comfortable."

Note that. "Confident" and "comfortable" were the words Harris used. That provides a clear message about gun selection.

Of course, Drury also likes other features in a turkey gun.

"I like to use optics (a scope) because they're a logical match with today's tight chokes and efficient shotshells," he said. "I don't want any magnification because that can lead to taking shots that are too long. Just give me a 1-power scope using the red-dot system (he uses a Burris Speed Dot), and I have what I need."

Drury prefers shotguns with 24- to 28-inch barrels.

"I've found that the longer-barreled guns shoot slightly better," he said, "and although it isn't a factor with a scope, the longer sight plane of 26- or 28-inch barrels makes it less likely you'll shoot high if you aren't using optics. Right now, I'm using Remington's new 11-87 Super Magnum (an autoloader chambered for 3-inch shells)."

The gun is heavy enough to absorb plenty of recoil, and Drury believes reduced recoil helps accuracy. You don't want to think about a gun hurting you before you fire.

"Looks don't matter in a turkey gun, except that you want it to be camouflaged," Drury said with a laugh. "I like today's synthetic stocks with a dipped camo finish."

However, he said tape or other approaches to masking a gun also work.

Drury believes a turkey gun should feature a good, comfortable sling for long days afield when you walk, crawl, climb and shoulder your gun frequently. The gun must be tough and durable. The turkey woods are no place for a fancy shotgun.

Drury also wants his gun to have a quiet safety.

"This doesn't get the attention it should," he said. "I'm happy with a thumb or a finger safety, but I want one that can be pushed on or off with almost no noise. A loud click at a critical moment can ruin a hunt."

In final analysis, each Outland expert has particular preferences about turkey guns. However, they share much common ground, such as having faith in a gun and knowing its capabilities. By combining their thoughts and insights with your perspectives, you can intelligently select a turkey gun. If it performs efficiently and effectively, that's what's important.

PART II: LOADS

Although debate about the ideal turkey load has fewer nuances than arguments on guns, the subject inspires many differences. Some folks swear by No. 4 shot, but others are partial to No. 5, 6 or even 7½ shot. Further, some like duplex loads, although these aren't nearly as popular as they were several years ago.

No specific shot size works best all the time, and some thought should make that obvious. Large No. 4 shot carries a bit more energy and knockdown power, but you must sacrifice pellet numbers. Conversely, a swarm of No. 7½ shot might work best for close birds.

Other factors, such as buffering, powder loads and shot charges, complicate matters. Turkey hunting has become sufficiently popular to induce ammunition manufacturers to offer plenty of variety, and at least one major company, Winchester, did loads of hard research before introducing its Supreme turkey loads.

Hunters must also realize that there's something to be said for high-power loads not designed for turkeys. If you shoot an older gun chambered only for 2¾-inch shells, for example, you might have to rely on high-brass shotshells rather than turkey loads.

"Although it's been my observation that most factory guns shoot No. 4 shot best, you really need to find out what suits you and your gun best," Drury said. "There's the high energy of No. 4s, but No. 6s offer lots of pellets. With No. 5 shot, you sort of get the best of both worlds. Really, all these shot sizes, when combined with a suitable powder charge, have plenty of energy to kill a turkey."

"Just as I've tested a lot of guns with different attributes, I've spent a lot of time trying different loads and shot sizes," Harris said. "For the most part, I shoot No. 6 shot and have tried to find a gun that patterns well with them. I've even had quite a bit of success with No. 7½ shot, although when you use them, judging distance accurately to be sure the bird is close enough can be critical. I'm a fan of high-density patterns, and smaller shot sizes offer that."

As those remarks reveal, Drury and Harris also have specific preferences and subtle differences when it comes to loads. Again, though, they provide expert guidance from a wealth of practical experience. By taking advantage of their insight, you can determine which loads suit you and your gun — after paying your dues at the patterning range.

The outcome you seek — like Harris, Drury and every other turkey hunter — is a combination of gun and load that removes equipment-related uncertainty from your hunts.

84

Clothing
and Accessories

When reduced to essentials, turkey hunting need not be complex or involve significant expenses. Equipped with nothing more than a shotgun, shells, calls and clothing that lets you merge with your surroundings, you can succeed.

In fact, there's no denying that modern turkey hunters face many choices about acquiring gear. Just attend any late-winter sport show or the NWTF's annual national convention, and you'll find enough gadgets and gimmicks to plumb the depths of all but the most flush billfolds.

Sometimes, it seems turkey hunters rival bass fishermen. Just as the latter seek a foolproof lure, turkey hunters hope for an irresistible call or camouflage that renders them invisible.

Obviously, such things haven't — and never will be — made. Somehow, though, we keep hoping — and spending money. For now, let's set aside the hype, hoopla, marketing and mind games, and get to the nitty gritty of what you need while turkey hunting. Obviously, requirements differ somewhat. For example, where you live and hunt figures prominently in your choice of clothing, footwear and camouflage. Likewise, you must decide, based on circumstances, how much money you're willing to spend.

Recognizing those variations, though, advice from Mark Drury and Brad Harris can be invaluable. They have "been there, done that" when it comes to gearing up. They use gear and, in many cases, have designed products or originated concepts that led to the development of a new call or other equipment.

CLOTHING AND FOOTWEAR

"I'm a Mossy Oak man who's loyal to Toxey Haas and the various Mossy

Oak patterns," Drury said.

However, Harris has been a Realtree fan for a long time.

"I want something that blends with the surroundings where I hunt, and it works well for me," he said. "Bill Jordan has been a big supporter of mine from the outset."

What this indicates, obviously, is brand loyalty, something many hunters share with Harris and Drury.

"Most of the camouflage patterns on the market work, but I especially like the cut of Mossy Oak," Drury said.

His favorites include chamois, which he described as "built for hunters," and 100 percent cotton.

"One of the nice things about camouflage clothing today is that you can get what you need for almost any type of weather," he said. "During spring or even in a single hunt, you can have everything from temperatures below freezing to stifling heat and humidity. Whatever the situation, you want to be comfortable."

Drury also advocates layering.

"It's easy enough to remove a shirt or two and stuff them in your vest," he said. "By peeling off a layer at a time, you can be comfortable on a frosty morning and remain that way when it gets quite warm later in the day."

Harris also mentioned comfort as a critical factor for clothing.

"One feature I really recommend is cargo-style pants," he said. "Most hunters welcome the additional places to store gear. You want a fabric suited to the climate and weather conditions and a pattern that fits the country."

For example, Harris wears a net jacket over a camo T-shirt after the weather warms.

"Realtree offers me the variety I need as I travel to different parts of the country," he said.

Let's examine a couple of other considerations. Breathable long underwear feels good on cold, raw days, and in many parts of the country, raingear merits a place in your vest or vehicle. In areas where mosquitoes or ticks are prevalent, you might consider attire designed to deal with them. Keeping still while mosquitoes whine in your ear and do their darndest to suck your carcass dry, or concentrating on an old tom when ticks advance, takes more will than most of us possess.

Drury and Harris have also given considerable thought about other attire. For headgear, they like baseball-style caps.

HARRIS HAS BEEN A REALTREE FAN for a long time. "I want something that blends with the surroundings where I hunt, and it works well for me," he said. "Bill Jordan has been a big supporter of mine from the outset."

FOR HEADGEAR, Brad Harris and Mark Drury like baseball-style caps. "This type cap shades your eyes but doesn't impair your hearing," Harris said. "Brimmed hats cut down on your hearing ability a bit."

"This type cap shades your eyes but doesn't impair your hearing," Harris said. "Brimmed hats cut down on your hearing ability a bit."

"Baseball-type caps are tailor-made for turkey hunters," Drury said.

Their preferences for headnets differ, partly because Drury wears glasses and Harris doesn't.

"I like a three-quarter chameleon mask," Drury said. "But I don't like any mask with wires. I prefer form-fitting ones you can pull down around your neck when not in use."

Such designs also reduce the likelihood of losing a headnet, although it's wise to keep a spare in your vest.

"No matter what type of covering you use," Drury said, "I have a couple of hints that will help you avoid your glasses fogging up. Treat them before hunting with an anti-fogging spray, and be sure to breathe down from your mouth."

Typically, Harris likes a half-net or facemask with good-sized eye openings.

"I don't want my eyes covered," he said. "I want to be sure nothing obstructs my peripheral vision. I will go to a full headnet when mosquitoes are really bad."

Regarding gloves, Harris emphasizes feel.

"Some calls are difficult to run properly if you're wearing thick gloves and can really hamper your effectiveness," he said.

Drury's handwear is simple.

"I just buy brown jersey gloves," he said. "They're comfortable, inexpensive and you can find them anywhere. I'm always losing gloves, so I make a point of having an extra pair in my vest. In fact, I usually buy a dozen at a time."

If you're concerned about feel, you can cut off the fingertips of your gloves to obtain maximum sensitivity for tasks such as holding a striker.

Any turkey hunter who walks a lot knows foot comfort comes first. Wet feet on a cold day can leave you miserable. Ill-fitting boots can produce hotspots, blisters or worse. Insulated boots might help keep you warm instead of shivering during a lengthy setup. Inappropriate soles can make you slip and slide on steep slopes or contribute to a serious accident, such as one I experienced with a 10-foot fall onto rocks.

Also, in some situations, you must consider snake boots, threats posed by prickly pear cacti or similar vegetation, or colors that won't give you away. For most of their spring hunting, Harris and Drury agree about footwear.

"I usually wear LaCrosse Burleys," Drury said. "They're waterproof and offer good traction in mud, and I like the way they fit," he said. "They've always been my boots of choice when hunting in areas that are swampy, feature branches and small creeks or otherwise make it likely you'll encounter water."

Harris has also worn LaCrosse boots, along with Red Ball and other rubber footwear.

"Usually though, unless I'm in really wet terrain, I wear Rocky boots with Cordura uppers and a rubber bottom," he said. "They offer me good ankle support and are pliable yet rugged."

Drury also wears a Rocky product — Stalkers — in dry country.

"The key considerations to keep in mind are fit, function and a color that blends in," he said.

If you have difficulty finding ideal fits because of high arches, or wide or narrow feet, you can obtain made-to-order boots from Russell. No matter what boots you select, don't break them in while turkey hunting. Do it while mowing your lawn, working in the garden, or during short hikes or pre-season scouting forays.

For leather, I recommend softening and waterproofing treatments. Also, you might try something I learned during my soccer-playing days. I would stand in a shower wearing new leather footwear, get the shoes wet, and then wear them 30 to 45 minutes. As they began to dry, they would form-fit my feet. Afterward, treating the leather regularly was the key for comfort.

Socks are another critical comfort factor. You want clean ones, obviously. Probably the best way to avoid blisters is to keep them dry and wear two pairs. Many socks have wicking qualities that help avoid dampness and resultant blister-producing friction. Also, you can always change socks at midday, and carrying an extra pair of socks won't add much weight to your vest.

ACCESSORIES

A vest might be described as clothing or a piece of gear. It fits both bills, but however viewed, a vest is necessary. A good vest features ample carrying space, many specialized pockets, adjustable shoulder straps, padding for your back and butt, and maybe built-in support.

Harris and Drury like the latter quality and use vests by Bucklick Creek. Drury calls Bucklick's Turkey Lounger "the ultimate turkey vest," and Harris "likes its features." The Bucklick Creek design offers an internal support frame that lets you sit comfortably even when a tree or other back rest isn't available.

"The key consideration with any vest is organization," Harris said. "You want pockets to handle lots of calls and locators, and it helps if they're the right shape to handle box calls, slates and what have you. Good, tight shell loops are another nice feature."

Drury believes a fold-down seat is another critical feature.

"I prefer this to separate cushions or inflated doughnuts," he said, "because it is always ready and one less thing to remember."

Other hunters prefer lightweight portable seats, which give them a bit of elevation and lessen discomfort during long sessions at one spot. Offsetting these attributes are bulkiness and a bit of extra weight.

When selecting a vest, also consider the shape and carrying capacity of the back pouch. The best models let you easily carry a turkey and have button-up designs that ensure you won't lose decoys or clothing. A water-proof internal coating is also a plus, because it keeps water from oozing in or

BINOCULARS ALLOW YOU TO CHECK the ground ahead when in doubt, and obviously they're useful for scouting and finding distant turkeys.

turkey blood from leaking.

You'll likely store most of your accessories in a vest. What those include varies by preference and, somewhat, the area you're hunting.

"I always carry lots of calls along with several locators," Harris said. "Then I'll have a compass to help me course turkeys or find my way when hunting areas I don't know well, red ribbon for marking purposes (make sure you remove it after it has served its purpose) and a flashlight."

His vest also contains other items, including binoculars.

"They let you check the ground ahead when in doubt, and obviously they're useful in scouting and finding distant turkeys," he said. "I usually carry two and often three decoys, with one of them being a jake. A bottle of water will add some weight, but it can really be welcome on hot days or when you walk a lot."

Incidentally, wingbone calls sound better if you occasionally suck water through them as you would a straw.

"I don't eat while hunting, but many folks like to carry trail mix, a candy bar or some sort of snack," Harris said. "I also carry a pen for filling out tags, a length of slender rope, and a hunting knife I wear on my belt and

Gerber Multipliers. I don't carry a turkey tote. Instead, I'll put a bird in my vest or make a carrier by cutting a stick with my knife and attaching a piece of rope to it."

Harris likes multipliers, which regularly serve various needs afield.

"I might use the pliers to work on a call, my gun or its sling or maybe something else," he said.

Harris supplements his compass when hunting new territory by carrying U.S. Geological Survey topographical maps and notes,

"I'll occasionally use a Global Positioning System unit in those circumstances," he said. "Also, if you have doubts about where you have roosted a bird or your ability to relocate a promising strut zone, a GPS can be a real asset.

"Finally, I can't imagine any turkey hunter being without clippers. They're useful for building blinds or getting bushes out of the path of your gun when you set up. But the way I probably use shears the most is to clip briars or other things while I'm slipping along."

Drury agreed.

"Clippers are a must for me," he said. "With them, I can make sure I clear out a good view for shooting with a video camera and the gun. If the situation dictates staying in the same spot for a long time, or if the logical setup leaves me exposed, building a good blind takes only a couple of minutes as you clip limbs or brush and stick it in the ground."

Drury's accessories resembles Harris' with one interesting addition — knee pads.

"You can't beat the sort of knee pads cement workers and others use," he said. "They let you get down and cover some distance in relative comfort. You don't have to worry about briars, cactus thorns or sharp rocks, and in the kind of hunting I do, you'll often find some creeping and crawling becomes essential."

Drury also emphasizes decoys.

"Decoys can be your best friends when videoing a hunt," he said. "In effect, they let you position the turkey, if he decides to come, in a way that makes filming possible. I carry a hen and a jake, the newly popular breeding pair (True Position Breeders from Feather Flex). Later in the season, when the peak of the breeding cycle has passed, I might use a single jake and a single hen."

In addition to the gear mentioned by the Outland experts, you should

MARK DRURY AND BRAD HARRIS AGREE on the importance of clippers. "I can't imagine any turkey hunter being without clippers," Drury said. "They're useful for building blinds or getting bushes out of the path of your gun when you set up."

A Turkey Hunter's Gear Checklist

Most of these items have been covered in this chapter, but listing them together might prove useful as you scramble, the night before opening day, to make sure everything is ready. Not all of these items are essential, but they can serve as reminders as you pick and choose what you'll carry.

➤ Camouflage clothing

➤ Vest

➤ Boots

➤ Socks

➤ Shotgun

➤ Shotgun shells

➤ Flashlight

➤ Compass

➤ Decoys and stakes

➤ Turkey calls

➤ Locator calls

➤ Turkey tote

➤ Pruning shears

➤ Hunting knife

➤ Raingear

➤ Headnet or facemask

➤ Gloves

➤ Cap or hat

➤ Binoculars

➤ Rangefinder

➤ Camera and film

➤ Choke tubes and wrench

➤ Seat or cushion

➤ First-aid kit

➤ Water bottle

➤ Snacks

➤ Pen (to fill out tags)

➤ GPS

➤ Topographical maps

➤ Gallon Ziploc bags for holding turkey giblets. These can also be used to protect slate and box calls during rainy weather

➤ Portable blind or camouflage cloth for making a blind

➤ Insect repellent

➤ Lanyards for wing-bone calls, tube calls or locators

➤ Marker ribbon or limb-lights to help you relocate a roost site

➤ Knee pads

carry other accessories, including a camera, insect repellent, a basic first-aid kit, and at least four or five shotshells. Beyond that, let preference guide you. Just as a back-country camper considers every ounce of weight that goes into his pack, analyze each piece of gear that enters your vest, weights down your pockets or hangs from your belt.

In the long run, experience might be your best teacher. If you encounter a situation where a missing accessory becomes an immediate need, you won't forget it again. However, I'd bet most hunters have an item or two they have handled only when they clean out their vests.

"Make absolutely sure you have everything you use or might reasonably expect to use," he said. "Beyond that, I wouldn't recommend carrying it — it's just excess baggage."

Dress sensibly, and plan carefully in terms of accessories. Meet the rigid standards of preparedness while ensuring comfort. By doing that, you increase your chances of success and make sure you will enjoy the hunting experience. These considerations are sound arguments for devoting regular attention to gear. Maintain it, replace items — or acquire new ones — as necessary, and always go afield appropriately dressed and suitably outfitted. It's a hallmark of an accomplished turkey hunter.

The Wonders of Woodsmanship

I grew up in the tiny North Carolina mountain town of Bryson City, where the dean of American campers, Horace Kephart, lived for the final 27 years of his life. His enduring book *Camping and Woodcraft*, one of the best-selling outdoors books of all time, was my bedside companion as a youngster. It remains a source of abiding wisdom and consultation, and offers the sage advice, "In the school of the woods, there is no graduation day."

New lessons abound in the turkey's haunts, and as you advance through each step of a never-ending curriculum, the education affords moments of simple pleasure and self-discovery. Better still, you become a more capable, accomplished hunter. In time, the truth in the turkey hunting adage, "Calling is 10 percent and woodsmanship 90 percent," becomes apparent.

The essence of woodsmanship is experience. Your mind accumulates and assimilates information, and you, like a scientist performing experiments in a laboratory, use reason to make deductions. You learn, for example, that turkeys typically leave their roosts later and fly up earlier during rainy days. Also, you see that during similar conditions, turkeys prefer open fields. They might be exposed to the elements, but it keeps them clear of a potentially dangerous situation where they can't hear well, and where the wind creates so much movement that they can't see to their advantage. Those are just two examples of the wisdom skilled hunters will have stored in their treasure houses of knowledge.

To a degree, you must be in the woods to learn woodsmanship, although reading about it can provide a base upon which to build. Likewise, a seasoned mentor who shares information and insight accumulated during a lifetime afield can be a friend. I have been privileged in this regard. I got my start turkey hunting with Parker Whedon, who has dealt with gobblers for portions of seven decades. Also, because I write about turkey hunting, I have many chances to learn from today's finest hunters. Most are high-profile folks, including videographers, competition callers, seminar speakers, pro staffers for major call-making companies or combinations thereof. However, you'll find scores of equally capable turkey hunters who remain unknown beyond their home areas. Often, this is by choice, because the old-time secrecy associated with turkey hunting endures.

Yesterday's skilled turkey hunters invariably became accomplished through countless hours of effort, and turkey numbers were so low that they were reluctant to share what they knew. Who can blame them? Why give away something you spent a lifetime amassing, unless you passed it down to someone you loved or greatly respected?

Nowadays, things have changed, thanks largely to the increase in turkey numbers and the sport's commercialization. No longer do skilled hunters have to worry about hoarding hard-earned acumen, because gobbler numbers are more than sufficient. For those professionally involved in turkey hunting, sharing is advantageous. The interest created or stimulated sells products.

What this should tell you, whether you're a novice or veteran, is you can find some shortcuts to becoming a better woodsman. Reading expert advice and watching instructional videos is one way. Another one is to find a teacher, a guru of gobbler insight, willing to teach you the ropes and share his secrets. This chapter attempts to do both. It lets you pick the brains of two first-rate woodsmen, fellows who have, in one way or another, contributed to the demise of hundreds of longbeards. Take my word, they hold nothing back. Admittedly, reading is no substitute for being there, but in the scouting and woodcraft lessons that follow, you can join Mark Drury and Brad Harris in studying several aspects of woodsmanship.

FINDING AND READING SIGN

The ability to read and analyze sign is part and parcel to being a turkey hunter.

"You should always be on the lookout for sign," Drury said.

Harris agreed.

"For a good turkey hunter, finding and evaluating sign becomes second nature," he said.

Because of his schedule, Drury doesn't get to do lots of nonhunting scouting.

ONE WAY TO LEARN about woodsmanship is to find a teacher willing to teach you the ropes and share his secrets. Here, Mark Drury, right, and Cecil Carder, left, show a student's results from a turkey school they offered in Texas.

"And that's one area where the average hunter often enjoys an advantage," he said. "There is no substitute for observed behavior, and as you learn things, use them."

You might not have to wait days or weeks to use such knowledge, although that might be true of pre-season observations. Harris and Drury constantly scout as they hunt.

"Sometimes, things can be tough the first day," Harris said. "But maybe you learn something that will help you the next day, and many times I get a bird on the second or third day after failing the first. Often, that results from things I learned the first day."

That is, woodsmanship is a constant, integral part of the tools and attitude the Outland experts use in turkey hunting.

The world's finest woodsmen, the Bushmen of southern Africa and the aborigines of the remote Australian outback, can unerringly track an animal over even the rockiest surfaces. The tracking skill of Bushmen almost transcends belief. They can shoot a giant animal, such as an eland, with a tiny poisoned arrow — after getting within 15 yards of it — and then track it for miles during two or three days until the slow-acting poison takes effect. Such skills come from necessity and training at a young age that lasts a lifetime.

Turkey hunters can never hope to attain such skill, but it's a warming thought to hold while learning the ways of the woods.

Sign falls into various categories, but it always provides what you seek: evidence that turkeys are present. After you find that evidence, you must determine what it means. It seems simple, but that's not always true. For example, finding where turkeys have scratched is one thing. Determining when that scratching was done, how many turkeys did it and the sex of those birds is another.

Physical evidence — feathers and droppings — forms a logical starting point. Breast feathers let you ascertain a bird's sex because gobbler feathers have solid black edges. However, feathers are ephemeral, and a good rain usually beats them into the ground.

"You often find breast feathers near a dusting site," Drury said. "If you find feathers where turkeys have clearly dusted recently, it isn't a bad place to do some calling. Even if you see nothing but hen feathers, chances are good that during the mating season, there's a gobbler nearby."

Primary wing- and tailfeathers last longer, but they can be less helpful in determining strategy.

"But if you find two or three broken wingfeathers, maybe mixed with smaller feathers, it might be evidence of a recent fight between two gobblers," he said. "That's the sort of thing a hunter wants to know, because he knows there are birds present and that they've been sorting out the pecking order."

Finding a pile of feathers is bad news because it means another predator — a bobcat, coyote or another hunter — has killed a bird.

Feathers and droppings together usually indicate a roost site, and if droppings are plentiful, the location has likely been used regularly. I've seen piles of droppings several inches deep in New Zealand, examined roosts in Texas where Rio Grandes flocked like the trees were a turkey motel, and seen trees where Merriam's had for years roosted night after night. Easterns and Osceolas will also use the same roost sites, although not as commonly as Rios and Merriam's. They have more options to choose from, which partially explains this behavior.

When examining a suspected roost, it's easy to distinguish between hen and gobbler droppings. Hen droppings have a conical or round shape, but a gobbler's fecal matter is elongated and often J-shaped.

Also, examine the freshness of droppings. If scat is steaming hot, a bird just left the area. If the excrement resembles a chalky fossil, it's ancient. Of course, climate dictates how rapidly droppings dry. The same holds true for scratching.

Evidence of where turkeys have been feeding means more to a fall hunter than a spring hunter. However, it's always significant.

"Leaves raked back, cow pies turned over, scratching in newly plowed ground or raking in a chufa patch tell you turkeys are present," Drury said.

After you find scratching, try to age it.

"If the ground is still damp where leaves have been raked back, or if the soil is dark when the crust around it is dry, you know turkeys have been feeding quite recently," Harris said.

Much the same holds true for tracks. If they are crisp and defined — with moisture in the bottom of ones on a sandbar or wrinkles from the pads on the bottom of a turkey's foot still discernible — tracks were likely made that day. Similarly, if strut marks where a turkey has dragged his wings are defined, they're recent. If they're blurred and indistinct, they have weathered two or three days of wind, several nights of dew or maybe a light shower.

You can easily distinguish between hen and gobbler tracks because tom tracks are appreciably longer and wider. Incidentally, although this book doesn't include a detailed examination of track size or similar matters, Lovett Williams' 1989 book *The Art and Science of Wild Turkey Hunting* contains much of this information.

"Tracks can do much more than tell you whether they were left by a gobbler or a hen," Harris said. "You can determine if the turkey was walking or running by the distance between tracks, whether he was moving from one location to another or just rambling, and whether the prints were left by a single bird, a gobbler following a hen, two toms traveling together or a group of jakes. Knowing that sort of thing and being able to read tracks can help a hunter a great deal."

Drury offered similar advice for strut marks.

"The presence of a lot of strut marks, especially if they seem to have been made at different times, tells you a lot," he said. "Where it's obvious a gobbler has done a lot of displaying, pirouetting and dragging the ground through quite an area, you know this is a preferred strutting zone. Anytime I locate such an area, particularly if I have several days to hunt, I have infor-

OFTEN, A DISTANT OBJECT will catch your eyes. You can ease up your binoculars and check it before moving.

Brian Lovett

mation that can be quite useful. I know the gobbler is likely to make further visits, and if I should strike a turkey in the general area, I know the zone is a place he would be comfortable."

More sign indicates more turkeys. However, a dearth of sign doesn't mean you should give up. Some types of ground, for example, don't readily show tracks, and you can easily miss droppings in grass that's a few inches high. A hunt I shared with Drury several years ago in South Carolina provides a good example.

We had not roosted a bird the previous evening. Dawn brought no gobbling, and there was no sign. By 8 a.m., Drury said, "I don't believe there are any turkeys here." I was inclined to agree. However, 90 minutes later, after a classic yo-yo calling contest with a group of gobblers, we were shaking hands over a fine tom, the finale of which had been captured on camera.

Even when you don't see lots of sign, you never know for sure. In some cases, you must take the geographical hand you have been dealt. No matter the circumstances, you should constantly search for and evaluate sign.

USING YOUR SENSES

One of the few specifics I recall from first grade involves safety when crossing a street: "Stop, look and listen." That also holds true for turkey hunters.

From the moment you leave your vehicle until your gun has been cased at the day's end, you must be constantly alert. You won't smell a turkey, just as they can't smell you. However, use the senses that also serve the turkey — sight and sound — to your advantage.

Obviously, you must be alert for turkey sounds, vocal or otherwise. Listen for and learn to identify turkey talk, and the sounds of birds flying, gobblers fighting, spitting and drumming, birds walking or scratching or wingtips dragging through dry leaves.

Harris said other sounds can also indicate turkeys are present.

"Crows making a persistent fuss can mean that they are looking at a turkey," he said. "Also, if a squirrel suddenly starts barking nearby, especially after you have been set up for a while and know you haven't done anything to stir up the bushytail, he might see a turkey. It could also be a deer or something else, but you want to pay attention to the direction where the racket comes from."

Also, remain aware of the whereabouts of other gobblers, even when you work a specific bird.

"I try to pinpoint the position of those other gobblers because odds are, I'll need them," Drury said. "If I hear distant birds on the roost when I've set up on one nearby, I might want to hunt them tomorrow or check if I can roost one at the end of the day. If things don't work out with the first bird, they offer backup opportunities."

It's easier to hear turkeys when you're still. When moving, ease along, and pause often to listen. Don't rush from place to place like a hyped-up bass fisherman who cruises into promising structure, makes a dozen casts, and then guns the motor to repeat the performance elsewhere.

"I like to cover a lot of ground, but you have to cover it wisely," Drury said. "That means a lot of listening, and don't fail to use your eyes."

Often, a distant object will catch your eye. You can ease up your binoculars and check it before moving. Closer movement deserves careful scrutiny. For every gobbler you see easing in silently, there will be dozens of birds, squirrels and deer. Still, the sudden appearance of a tail fan over a ridgetop or a patch of red where it hadn't been before can send shock waves through your system.

SCOUTING

Looking for turkeys — scouting — involves your eyes and ears, although the former dominate. As we have seen, scouting is a constant, unending process. It occurs during the hunt and before the season.

"Also, you can do some meaningful scouting during deer season," Drury said. "Turkeys won't be in the same places in spring as fall, but they will have the same general range. If you spot several longbeards while sitting in a stand in fall, they will be somewhere within a mile or so come greening-up time."

That brings up another aspect of scouting: the importance of being able to recognize turkeys' favored food sources, roost sites, nesting areas, dusting spots and other places they use. In spring, turkeys focus on greenery, insects, chufas and grain left from winter or planted in spring. As spring progresses and the landscape becomes increasingly green, moving from south-facing slopes and creek bottoms to the entire landscape, turkeys might feed in a wider area.

"I'm always scouting and trying to read sign," Harris said. "I always have a pair of binoculars in my truck. Everything kicks into overdrive a few weeks before the season opens. Then, I do a lot of walking and use locator calls a lot."

The worst thing you can do is yield to the temptation — it's powerful — and use turkey calls before the season. It proves nothing and gives gobblers a graduate course in avoidance therapy.

Harris also keeps a notebook in his truck.

"I'll make notes of things such as roost areas or places where I see gobblers strutting regularly," he said. "You can never have enough birds located."

Harris and Drury also scout during off-hours (hunting in Missouri ends at noon or 1 p.m., depending whether daylight-saving time has kicked in). The time immediately before fly-up can be especially useful.

WEATHER WISDOM

Devoted hunters seldom let adverse weather interfere with their hunting, but there's no denying that weather dramatically affects turkey behavior. This list includes tidbits of weather wisdom from the Outland experts, with some of my observations thrown in.

➤ Turkeys prefer open areas when it's rainy or windy.

➤ Distant thunder often produces shock-gobbles.

➤ Turkeys often tune up when warm sun follows a sudden shower or thunderstorm.

➤ After extended bad weather, turkeys gobble well when a front moves out and sun returns.

➤ Turkeys sometimes stay on the roost late when it rains hard or steadily.

➤ Turkeys roost lower on windy nights, and they roost away from the prevailing wind.

➤ Calm, cool mornings seem to produce intense gobbling.

➤ Turkeys gobble less frequently in adverse weather.

➤ Loud, penetrating calls can be an asset during windy days.

➤ When it's so windy you have trouble keeping decoys in place, consider cutting sticks to place on each side of the fakes.

➤ When the wind blows steadily and hard, hunt low, sheltered areas.

OTHER ASPECTS OF WOODCRAFT

Although this quality defies description or analysis, the finest woodsmen can do more than perform the above-mentioned considerations. They possess an ability — call it a sixth sense, extrasensory perception or whatever you like — to know things will happen before they do. They feel the presence of a bird. Harris compared this skill to one some veterans developed in Vietnam.

"They sensed when things were wrong, when an ambush was imminent or when trouble was in the offing," he said.

The finest woodsman I've known served three tours of duty as a sniper in Vietnam. Walking through the woods with him was eerie. When I walked in front of him, I constantly peeked over my shoulder to see if he was still there. He was that quiet.

He also knew the woods with rare intimacy. That's not the lot of an average hunter, and most experienced turkey hunters will, if pressed, confess they have at some time been lost. Even the ultimate American woodsman, at least according to folklore and legend, experienced that problem. When someone asked Daniel Boone if he had ever gone astray, he replied, "I've never been lost, but I was once temporarily misplaced for three days."

The solution, of course, is to carry a compass or GPS unit. Forget old saws about moss on the northern sides of trees and similar stuff. Carry a compass. As we've seen, it can help course turkeys and can be a source of comfort if you get turned around or "temporarily misplaced."

FOR CONSISTENT SUCCESS, you must take a page from the old-timers. Almost without exception, they were fine woodsmen. "Woodsmanship is still the No. 1 attribute of a really good hunter," Harris said.

FINAL THOUGHTS ON WOODSMANSHIP

A good woodsman invariably deserves the description of "hard hunter." Tenacity kills turkeys, and hunters who end every day afield dog tired and bone weary have more than their share of triumphs. This persistence also helps you develop a knowledge of and feel for the woods. Dogged determination, the will to win and a solid work ethic figure in the making of a woodsman.

"He knows the woods and appreciates nature, and he's always interpreting," Harris said. "He moves through the woods quietly and confidently."

After Harris offered that thought, he started laughing so hard he almost choked. When I asked why, he said our conversation reminded him of something his grandfather had said: "Brad, you can pass gas through a straw and kill a turkey when he's really hot."

Most hunters occasionally encounter that type of bird. For consistent success, however, you must take a page from the old-timers. Almost without exception, they were fine woodsmen. When turkeys were scarce, they had to be experts in woodcraft. Those qualities remain important. Turkey hunting's current time of plenty is no excuse to give woodsmanship a wink and a nod.

"Woodsmanship is still the No. 1 attribute of a really good hunter," Harris said.

Drury agreed.

"You frequently hear words to the effect that a fine woodsman who calls poorly will kill turkeys, while a superior caller who lacks basic woodcraft skills won't," he said. "That's accurate. Brad and I have had our share of success in competition calling, but that isn't what makes us hunters. Woodsmanship means much more."

Woodsmanship coupled with superior calling is like a fine pointer that also retrieves well. It's the icing atop the cake and the lace on the bride's pajamas.

Section 3
Tactics and Techniques

Finding Birds

An old-timer I know has two favorite turkey hunting adages.

"You can't get 'em if you can't find 'em," and "You ain't got a gobbler until you've got your foot on his neck or your hand on his feet."

Few would argue those pithy, plainspoken thoughts. No matter how well you can call and how well you're equipped, you cannot deny the importance of locating turkeys.

Scouting and woodsmanship obviously figure prominently in finding turkeys. Scouting, in effect, is a turkey hunter's long-range business plan. When properly done, it's as cold and calculating as anything in turkey hunting. Maybe poet Robert Burns had that in mind when he wrote,

"The best laid schemes o' mice and men,

Gang aft a-gley,

And leave us naught but grief and pain,

For promised joy."

When everything works, though, all that pre-season planning and preparation results in that little-used accessory, the turkey tote, getting a welcome dusting off as you remove it from the forgotten recesses of your vest. Then, "promised joy" becomes reality.

Finding birds involves scouting's basic skills. The only difference is immediacy. You want to locate birds quickly. To do so, you must use specific woodsmanship skills. Woodcraft is a composite of many elements, not all of which figure immediately in finding birds. However, certain aspects of woodsmanship go hand-in-hand with locating turkeys.

You can find turkeys three basic ways, and good hunters regularly use all these. They are associated with sight and sound. With the latter, however, locating involves distinct sounds: turkey vocalizations and nonvocal noises,

111

such as wingbeats, drumming, scratching and walking. Let's examine these, and then turn to Drury and Harris for pointers.

LOCATING BY SIGHT

The ability to recognize sign and, more important, analyze its age and the sex of the turkeys that made it, is paramount. A seasoned turkey hunter constantly looks for sign, studying the ground like an artifact enthusiast searching plowed bottom land after a rain. Incidentally, many fine turkey hunters have an uncanny knack for finding arrowheads and the like.

Finding good sign doesn't equate to locating a gobbler, but it often comes close. Locating signposts leaves you one step from finding gobblers. A prime example is a strut zone that shows obvious indications of regular, recent use. If you cannot find a vocal bird early in the morning, or the tom you attempt to call in is henned up, it's not a bad idea to spend midday near that active strutting area.

That's also true for a dusting spot that indicates turkeys have been there daily. Before setting up at a dusting spot, however, you might want to confirm gobblers have used the area. Breast feathers, nearby gobbler tracks or fresh tom droppings provide proof.

Another locating approach, which also involves sight, is glassing for distant gobblers. In the right terrain and with sufficient elbow room, this works well. In hill country, for example, especially spots with plenty of open pastures or fields, creeping to a ridge crest and carefully sweeping the ground below with binoculars can work better than calling. After you see a turkey and identify it as a gobbler, you can analyze the situation and move to a good setup before calling.

This also lets you determine immediately whether a tom has hens, and you can then decide whether to fool with the gobbler or seek a solitary bird.

Even if you decide to match wits with a henned-up gobbler, you know the situation in advance and can plan your attack. For example, you might study the direction in which the gobbler and his harem are drifting before moving closer and setting up.

You have two basic options for visually locating birds. The easiest involves traveling back roads, logging roads, pasture passages and the like by vehicle. Watch for telltale black balls in the distance, which might be strutting turkeys. Turkeys seem to pay little attention to distant vehicles, and in farm or ranch situations, where they see vehicles daily, they pay scant

ANOTHER LOCATING APPROACH that also involves sight is glassing for distant gobblers. In the right terrain and with sufficient elbow room, this works well.

heed if trucks keep moving. When you are several hundred yards away — or farther — turkeys might tolerate a vehicle stopping. Don't try that when they're close, though. Instead, keep going until you're out of sight, and then leave the vehicle and sneak back to watch the turkeys and figure out the situation.

The second option involves legwork, and in many places is the only option. You can use overgrown fencerows, ridgelines, ditches, dense brush, cane brakes, ground undulations and similar features to your advantage. Ease along carefully, looking and listening. Before stepping into an opening, such as a field or stretch of hardwoods with little understory, study the situation carefully. If a gobbler spots something even vaguely suspicious, it doesn't need a second opinion. It will close shop and depart.

In such situations, move quietly and carefully. You might not see like a sharp-eyed old tom, but binoculars or a spotting scope can help level the visual playing field. Steady attention to stealth also helps, and there's much satisfaction in seeing a bird at close range without disturbing it. Also, as I mentioned before, any time you find a gobbler visually, you enjoy flexibility.

You haven't called or alerted the tom of your presence, so you can decide the best approach without worrying about a longbeard suddenly deciding to make a move to where he heard calling.

LOCATING TURKEYS BY SOUND:
NONVOCAL APPROACHES

One of the finest attributes a hunter can have is acute hearing. Often, that's not the case, thanks to countless rounds fired at doves, clay pigeons or other targets without hearing protection. If you have suffered some hearing loss, however, you can find equipment, such as Walker's Game Ear, that helps. Still, the ability to hear and identify drumming, wingbeats, scratching, walking, fighting and other nonvocal turkey sounds can be helpful.

Spitting and drumming are undoubtedly the most elusive turkey sounds. You must be fairly close to hear them, and even then, uninitiated or inexperienced hunters often fail to discern these subtle noises, which almost seem to be at the edge of human hearing capacity. Conversely, hunters often convince themselves they hear a strutting bird when that's not the case.

It almost embarrasses me to admit, but years ago at Alabama's famed White Oak Plantation, I wasted half an afternoon listening to a boom box I thought was a turkey drumming. I could barely detect the bass vibrations from the noisemaker, and only after I finally moved toward the noise — after three hours of expecting a gobbler to appear momentarily — did I realize how foolish I had been.

Another time, I accompanied two good friends, neither of whom had killed a gobbler before, on a hunt. We walked into the midst of several roosted birds before daylight, discovering that only after distant thunder produced a half-dozen gobbles 70 or 80 yards from us. Hastily whispering that we needed to set up there, I somehow managed to situate my friends in front of me — I retreated about 40 yards — without disturbing the birds. A half-hour later, after calling softly and hearing the birds fly down, I heard drumming from the direction of the hunter to my right. It continued nonstop for 45 minutes before fading. Later, when I described the noise and asked him whether he had heard it, he said, "Yeah, I heard something like that, but I thought it was a generator running way off in the distance."

Probably the best way for uninitiated hunters to tune in on drumming is by listening as a bird struts. After you learn to detect spitting and drumming, you should always be alert for it in the turkey woods. When you hear it, find a setup with the urgency that a soldier seeks a foxhole after hearing, "Incoming." You can seldom hear drumming farther than 100 yards, and usually a longbeard will be closer.

Hearing turkeys walking or scratching can also help. These sounds carry well when leaves are dry. A turkey walking steadily through the woods sounds remarkably like a man, and that sends two messages. First, don't dismiss such sounds with disgust, thinking another hunter has intruded. It might be a gobbler seeking a hen. However, safety concerns dictate that it could be a hunter. Either way, be on high alert.

Scratching sounds similar, but it tends to be sporadic rather than steady. Also, even in spring, you'll often hear several turkeys scratching instead of one. Nonetheless, don't think it's nothing but a group of hens or jakes. Where you find hens during spring, you'll also likely find gobblers, and you cannot know which gender is scratching until you see the birds.

Fighting turkeys make a terrible racket, including raucous fighting purrs. However, you'll also hear clashing wings, and you should at least be able to recognize sounds of a struggle. These fights occur at any time of year, and both sexes fight. In spring, however, combat usually involves jakes or mature gobblers.

Wingbeats are perhaps the most useful nonvocal sound. Except when alarmed or crossing barriers, turkeys seldom fly during the day. However, when they fly up to roost at dusk, they make plenty of noise. It takes considerable effort — and noise — for a heavy bird to get airborne, and that's often magnified by wings clipping limbs on the way up. Also, turkeys seldom seem satisfied with their first perch. Often, they adjust several times to new limbs or other trees. Each time they adjust, you can hear it from a long distance.

Fly-down sounds are typically quieter. In the right situation, such as a roost tree at a field edge, a turkey might only require a couple of wingbeats to glide into the open. Still, a knowing ear can detect this.

The best place to listen for turkeys going to or leaving the roost is from an elevated position, such as the point of a finger ridge, a bluff overlooking a river bottom or a main ridge line with likely roosts on either side. Hearing flying birds at dawn or dusk gives you a starting point to focus on. At dawn, you'll also usually hear gobbles. Even so, it helps substantially to know a bird is on the ground. If nothing else, that might dictate switching from tree yelps to more aggressive calling.

It's wise to greet nightfall at a strategically chosen spot. Sometimes, nothing can induce a tom to gobble in the evening, but hearing birds fly to roost helps you know where you want to be come daylight.

Here's one more point about flying turkeys: Although it takes practice, you can, in time, distinguish between hen and gobbler wingbeats. Mature gobblers have slower, heavier wingbeats and typically make more noise, doubtless because of their greater bulk, when settling on a limb or taking off.

THOUGHTS ON LOCATING
FROM THE EXPERTS

Harris believes energy and enthusiasm can be your best allies for finding turkeys.

"I want to cover a lot of ground and locate as many turkeys as possible any time I hunt," he said. "That gives me the best odds. Some — maybe most — of those birds might shock-gobble only once or respond halfheartedly while sticking close to a bunch of hens. But if you give yourself the best odds, positive things are more likely to happen."

Harris said an integral part of consistently locating turkeys is "knowing which birds will work." Turkeys are so plentiful in many areas that they regularly respond to calling or gobble at dawn. However, that doesn't translate to a bird you can work in the fashion often described as "having a good hunt."

Occasionally, Harris will leave a bird — especially if he learns it has hens — to seek another.

"I can always come back later in the day and have a good chance of locating him again," he said. "Meanwhile, I always hustle. You can't be satisfied, and you can never locate enough turkeys. What you're seeking is the bird that's right at that moment. You've got to be confident to leave a bird, but if you believe in your ability to locate others — and a good work effort will contribute to that self-confidence — I believe you will find more."

Harris also believes you can dovetail information from scouting when locating turkeys.

"If you did your homework properly, you know quite a bit about the habits and routines of the turkeys you are hunting," he said. "Use that to your advantage in terms of where you use locator calls, where you set up, where you listen for birds and the like."

Harris is also convinced that you must be unpredictable.

"I WANT TO COVER a lot of ground and locate as many turkeys as possible any time I hunt," Harris said. " Some — maybe most — of those birds might shock-gobble only once or respond halfheartedly while sticking close to a bunch of hens. But if you give yourself the best odds, positive things are more likely to happen."

TIME IS OF THE ESSENCE when roosting. There's a magical period, usually a window of a quarter-hour or so, when a gobbler is most likely to gobble.

"Don't get in a rut," he said. "Be willing to try new locating techniques. This might involve using a new locator call, traveling a different path through familiar terrain or something else. It's just as important to be flexible as it is to be consistently unsatisfied. You've got to be hungry, and one of hunting's great thrills is to locate a willing gobbler."

Drury emphasizes roosting.

"I roost aggressively," he said. "It's an art. Knowing where a gobbler is and being able to analyze a situation can give you the sort of advantage you constantly seek.

"Time is of the essence when roosting. There's a magical period, usually a window of a quarter-hour or so, when a gobbler is most likely to gobble after he flies up in the evening. He's more likely to talk on the limb than on the ground."

No one knows why that's true, but it could be comfort, security, the desire to let nearby hens know his whereabouts or maybe a belligerent reminder that he's the boss

Whatever the case, Drury said he wants "to be in a prime spot — or maybe even try to get to two of them — in that time from sunset to dark."

"I try to learn the predictable roost spots on land I hunt regularly," he said. "Even in new territory, you can pick out places that might be preferred roosting areas."

Finding lots of fresh droppings sends an obvious message, but you should also recognize the prevailing wind direction, the presence of water — remember the adage about turkeys loving to hear their droppings hit water — or a patch of evergreens among still-barren hardwoods.

When hunting an area with several possible roosting sites, or when exploring uncharted territory, Drury likes to "roost and run." He might hit four or five locations, using a coyote howler or perhaps cutting loudly, to get a turkey to gobble. When a bird responds, the running part of Drury's act stops. If he or a partner can get the bird to gobble again, Drury attempts to close ground on the bird.

"I really like to get close, even locating the tree the bird is in or seeing the gobbler silhouetted in the fading light," he said. "Obviously you don't want to push things too much. You can get by with quite a bit more later in the season, thanks to the foliage. I consider 80 yards my ideal range, but you have to use common sense. After you reach a critical point where you feel uncomfortable with going farther, check things carefully."

"WHAT YOU'RE SEEKING is the bird that's right at that moment," said Drury. "You've got to be confident to leave a bird, but if you believe in your ability to locate others — and a good work effort will contribute to that self-confidence — I believe you will find more.

Drury believes that by doing this, you can determine where to set up at daylight. Some careful study helps him find his way back in the pre-dawn darkness.

"It's vital to avoid noise," he said, "and roosting is best done alone."

That also holds true when retracing your footsteps the next morning. If possible, you should be at your setup with decoys in place at least a half-hour before flydown.

Drury takes a scientific approach for reaching his set-up spot.

"I carefully count my steps on the way out," he said. "That tells me how many steps I need to make the next morning if I return the same way."

He also noted that it's "best to come from the west" in the morning. Obviously, the reverse holds true in the evening. Also, Drury said that if you must cross an open area in the morning, or if it's at or near a full moon, getting to your setup early is paramount.

If he doesn't roost a bird in the evening, Drury sticks with his basic concept.

"Getting close means a lot," he said. "Through the years, I've found that your odds of getting a bird to come to you from the roost are much higher when you are tight than when he's 200 yards away. Sometimes, you can get a bird to gobble long before daylight, and if that happens to me, I immediately begin trying to sneak close."

Whether just before dawn or just after dusk, you can enjoy the same advantage. A gobbler will be outlined against the light, but you will be a dark object against a dark background. Turkeys see movement in the dark, including deer and other creatures, all the time. However, whitetails don't make much noise.

"You can maybe get by with being seen if it's still quite dark," Drury said. "If you sound like an elephant, though, the turkey's going to be spooked."

Drury offered a closing thought derived from the heart of his hunting and call-making efforts.

"High pitch, whether in locator calls or turkey calls, helps you find turkeys," he said.

Harris also offered a final thought about locating birds.

"Expect the unexpected," he said. "You never know for sure where you might find a gobbler, so you always need to be alert and ready for action."

Tactics

The words tactics and strategy receive so much use in discussions about turkey hunting that you might assume you were at a military academy or army base.

That's understandable, because turkey hunting is a war of sorts. It involves a battle of wits, woodsmanship, calling ability and other skills, and in many ways, the battleground is uneven. The turkey is on home territory, and even a hunter intimately familiar with the lay of the land is at a disadvantage. Likewise, the turkey has everything to lose, and a hunter only stands to gain.

Webster's Dictionary defines tactics as, "Any method or procedure ... for accomplishing an end." The end turkey hunters seek is straightforward — killing a gobbler. In my opinion, hunting turkeys involves two considerations: tactics and calling. The other matters we've considered, including scouting, woodsmanship, guns and accessories, are preliminaries. They're essential, but the rubber meets the road with tactics and calling.

The term tactics covers almost everything a hunter does afield except working a turkey. This includes finding turkeys, but that subject is so important it was covered in the preceding chapter. For our purposes, tactics include selecting your line of approach, choosing a setup, setting up, repositioning when necessary and other maneuvers. Again, that's like a military term because dealing with a turkey, other than calling, is nothing more than a series of tactical maneuvers.

Unless you hire a guide, you must decide the appropriate tactics to deal with a gobbler. Usually, those decisions must be made quickly. After they're made, they must be implemented decisively. Your effectiveness as a turkey tactician will serve you better than advanced calling skills.

Tactics lie at the heart of turkey hunting. They form the sport's core, and you cannot overemphasize their importance. Acquiring tactical skills is a continuing process, and perhaps more than anything separates turkey hunting mediocrity from mastery. To some extent, you hone tactical skills through trial and error as you make mistakes, analyze them and try to avoid similar gaffes. The only problem is that every time the balance tips in the turkey's favor, you have again failed to grasp the golden ring atop the slippery slope of opportunity.

Sure, you should continue to profit from your mistakes. To do otherwise is foolish. However, the Outland experts acknowledge they have laundry lists of foul-ups dating back to boyhood, and they'll share invaluable insights from turkey hunting's school of hard knocks. Borrow from their experiences, and follow their advice. That can provide a significant shortcut as you travel the often rough, rocky but nonetheless rewarding road to success.

When quizzed about tactics, Drury answered quickly, suggesting he had given the issue significant thought.

"I have my own Big Four when it comes to tactics," he said. "They carry that rating because of what I have found works for me."

They include:

➤ Don't walk when you can drive. The more ground you cover, the more turkeys will hear your calling. Your odds improve with each turkey within hearing range of your calling or locator-calling. Go by truck, boat or bike, but cover ground. You'll have plenty of time afoot after you find a gobbler.

➤ Roost aggressively. That is extremely important.

➤ Have the right gun. That might seem more like a gear concern, but you gain a tactical advantage with a firearm you know well and that performs well.

➤ Use high pitch.

Harris' advice followed similar lines.

"I need to produce a lot of birds," he said, "because I'm always hosting writers or corporate guests. If not, I'm looking for new video footage. As a result, I'm very aggressive, and probably more than 80 percent of my hunting time is what I would characterize as a pushy or take-it-to-him mode."

Harris said his tactics preference dates back to the mid-1980s, when he started working on videos.

"By observing situations where everything had to be just right for the camera, I learned a lot that had escaped me when I was hunting and taking the first good shot," he said. "It became clear that calling can change a

"I NEED TO PRODUCE a lot of birds," Harris said, "because I'm always hosting writers or corporate guests. As a result, I'm very aggressive, and probably more than 80 percent of my hunting time is what I would characterize as a pushy or take-it-to-him mode."

"I CAN'T TELL my fellow hunters how important positioning is," Harris said. "You have to do everything you can to make it easy for the gobbler."

gobbler's mood, but I also learned a lot of other things that fall into the category of tactics."

Particularly, Harris advocates thinking about every situation and remembering that positioning is paramount.

"Hens move a lot, so you need to be willing to do the same," he said. "There's no doubt that you can sit in a blind all day and kill turkeys, but to me that isn't turkey hunting. I like to take the game to the gobbler, and that's an area where I'm aggressive that doesn't directly involve calling.

"I can't tell my fellow hunters how important positioning is. You have to do everything you can to make it easy for the gobbler, and one of the best ways to make it easy is to give him a short distance to travel and make that distance over ground where he feels comfortable."

That is, he recommends hunters think and move like a turkey. Be an analyst, and learn something from every encounter. In effect, after someone assumes he's a turkey-killing machine, a fall from grace is sure to follow. In turkey hunting, the old saw, "When you quit learning, it's time to quit," holds true.

One aspect of the learning experience Harris and Drury mentioned focuses on what could be described as accumulation of knowledge or a hunter's memory bank. After you have spent numerous days and springs in the woods, experiences run together. Ask any hunter who has killed 20 or more turkeys to recall and relive each hunt, and he likely won't be able to do it. That doesn't mean he has forgotten them, because he hasn't. Some prompting would likely bring back full, vivid recollections. However, a surer approach, which guarantees no lessons will escape you, involves keeping a tactical textbook. That could be a meticulously maintained diary, information on a computer hard drive or disk, or just notes you jot down after each hunt. When you kill a bird, you might keep the shotgun hull, and place the turkey's beard in it along with a slip of paper recording the details. No matter how you do it, reliving past hunts while relaxing in your armchair on a chilly winter day or when preparing for the season opener is interesting and instructional.

Beyond general thoughts about diaries and developing tactical knowledge, the two stratagems you must keep in mind involve approaching and setting up on turkeys, which occur after you have located a bird.

A turkey might be roosted, one that gobbled on its own or one that responded to locator or turkey calling. After you go as far toward the turkey as you dare, or as good sense and the terrain allow, you must select a position from which to work the bird. These topics deserve careful consideration.

MAKING THE APPROACH

Moving in on a turkey requires prudence and pushiness. The last thing you want to do is spook a longbeard — but you want to come to the brink before stopping. That's walking a tactical tightrope. At the outset, assuming you've heard a longbeard gobble instead of seeing it, judging distance is critical.

"Keep several things in mind when it comes to judging how far away a tom is," Drury said. "A bird facing away will sound like if he's much farther than when he turns in your direction and gobbles, and a bird that's still on the roost sounds closer than one on the ground. You also need to remember that wind or the lay of the land can alter the clarity with which you hear a gobble."

Harris provided similar thoughts.

"There are two things you can take to the bank when it comes to judging distance," he said. "If you can hear drumming, or a gobble seems to shake the ground, he's so close you need to get down immediately."

AFTER YOU HAVE TRAVELED as close to a turkey as common sense dictates, it's time to select a setup, get comfortable and start trying to work the bird within range.

Assuming a turkey isn't ultra-close, you'll want to get closer, and a compass can be useful. A quick compass reading — one of the wrist models or those on a watch band save precious seconds — can give you the precise direction to the bird. Then, several considerations enter the picture. If the turkey responded to yelping, he might be approaching. If possible, you should breach any barriers between you and the bird so the gobbler won't hang up. In hill or mountain country, you should try to set up above or at the same level as the bird. You can call a turkey downhill, but, for some reason, they prefer to move uphill.

At that time, Harris said, "Haste does not make waste." You must get into position quickly. You don't want to sound like a rampant hippopotamus on a 100-yard dash, but the quicker you can close the distance and set up, the better. As a rule of thumb, try to cut the distance between you and the bird in half. Judging that distance requires experience, and if you err, make sure it's on the side of caution.

Drury offered another helpful tip.

"The amount of foliage makes a real difference in how far you can hear a turkey," he said. "Late in the season in a wooded area with quite a bit of vegetation in the understory, when you hear a bird gobble on the ground, he won't be that far."

Getting closer to turkeys that gobble on their own or respond to a locator call is different. In those situations, you don't have to worry about the turkey coming to you as you go toward him. However, after you have covered a reasonable distance, it's wise to see whether you can get the bird to respond to a locator call. If the turkey gobbles, you can decide whether to move closer.

Another common situation involves gobblers in open areas. Longbeards love fields in spring. They can be seen — and see — from afar while strutting, and turkeys have extra security in fields. Turkeys adjourn to fields during rainy, windy days because weather-related noise hampers their hearing defenses, making sight more critical. Also, greening fields are favorite spring feeding areas. Field turkeys torment hunters, but you must deal with them. Drury's thoughts about field turkeys are interesting. After laughingly suggesting, "The best way to beat a field gobbler is with a rifle," he said you must focus on your approach.

"More often than not, you aren't going to call him out of the field," he said. "He'll gobble, but that's an invitation to you rather an announcement of an impending visit. You can't blame the gobbler. He has his harem, can be seen by any other hens who want to join him and feels safe and secure."

Drury believes the solution is a hunter's willingness to gain ground even in adverse conditions.

"Get out in the field with him," he said. "Creep, crawl, find a ditch, use a brush line or rely on undulations in the terrain. Do what it takes."

That assertiveness might be beneficial when things seemingly go wrong. It might spook a longbeard and his harem, get him out of the field and leave him lonely.

Another approach involves roosted birds. The art of roosting, including how to retreat after you have put birds to bed, was covered in the previous chapter. Just remember three things: Be sure about precisely where you want to go, be quiet as you get there, and get there plenty early.

No matter the type of approach, you'll reach a point where you must make a stand. After you have traveled as close to a turkey as common sense dictates, it's time to select a setup, get comfortable and start trying to work the bird within range.

SETTING UP

Setting up on a turkey seems simple. You select a spot from which to call, sit down and begin working the bird. In reality, as any turkey hunter knows, there's much more involved. Your set-up spot often decides whether a bird comes in. It figures — sometimes significantly — in how much patience you can exercise. Remaining in place when comfortable is different than being in agony, with roots reminding you of your last visit to the proctologist, or, as once happened to me, trying to keep still while fire ants feasted on my fanny. Also, you must consider overexposure, potential obstructions, sunlight vs. shadows, how well you are hidden, how far you can see and more.

"I'm always looking for setups as I walk through the woods, and before calling to locate a bird, it's always good to take a quick look around you," he said. "If a bird responds nearby and you don't really have much of a set-up spot, you can blow the whole deal."

Harris, who constantly mentions good positioning, said that's critical when it comes to setups.

"You need to be able to recognize promising set-up locations," he said, "and it should become almost second nature."

Always remember several basic set-up considerations. You don't want to be profiled, and if you can't find a tree that covers your body width, take special steps. A portable or quickly constructed blind can help. It blocks your outline — from the front rather than the rear — and serves the same purpose as a tree. Also, a blind lets you get by with extra movement, like running a call or repositioning for comfort, without being seen. However, blinds take time to construct. Also, they can restrict vision and sometimes provide a false sense of security that leads to mistakes or reduced vigilance.

One of the best times to use a blind is at a likely location during midday, when you intend to spend an hour or two in one spot. Also, blinds work well when you hunt near a food plot, or at the edge of a field or strutting zone. When you plan to remain in one spot for a long time, a blind makes sense.

Blind or no blind, you should always be well hidden when you set up. However, some hunters take that too far.

"You can get too well hidden," Drury said. "Being tucked down in a situation where you can only see for 30 yards or so works against you."

Conversely, it's wise, when possible, to avoid setups that let you see hundreds of yards (pastures or field edges are an exception). If you can see a long way, a turkey can too, and he has something like 20-10 vision to the fourth power.

In wooded ridge-and-valley country, Harris likes to set up where he can kill a gobbler when he first sees him.

"A good way to do this is to get in position 20 or 25 yards below a ridge line opposite from the direction in which you expect the bird to come," he said. "When his head pops over the horizon, you can shoot as soon as you get the gun on him."

As Harris mentioned, always consider a bird's expected line of approach when setting up. You want to make it easy for a gobbler to come to you. However, if a tom comes from an unexpected direction, you should be able to deal with him. Also, because a lovestruck gobbler wants to display, set up where he can strut his stuff. Drury offered a good example.

"If you call near an old road or trail, and a turkey answers on the other side of it, odds are excellent he will want to come to the road to strut," he said. "If you cross it to get closer to him, you may find that when you set up, he has gone to where you last called."

That dilemma crops up regularly and leads to another consideration — when to change positions.

You'll encounter several scenarios when you must change locations.

GETTING CLOSER TO TURKEYS that gobble on their own or respond to a locator call is different. In those situations, you don't have to worry about the turkey coming to you as you go toward him.

Sometimes, a turkey might respond regularly but steadily travel away. He might have hens with him and lead you down a futile chase, but if he's the only gobbler going, it's probably wise to follow.

"If a turkey is clearly going in the other direction, I'll often try to get in front of where he seems to want to be," Harris said. "If a bird seems like he's on a mission, you probably aren't going to change his mind."

Through repositioning, though, you might get where a gobbler feels more comfortable, or give him the impression the hen must be interested because she changed locations and tried to join him.

"It's a lot easier to work a bird from in front of him than behind," Drury said.

Harris said you must make sure the bird has left before changing your setup.

"Sometimes, you hear a turkey gobble 60 yards away, then the next time he's farther, and then he comes closer again, you probably have a bird in a strut zone," he said. "The time to make your move is when he's at the most distant point in the strut zone."

Drury also cautioned against leaving a setup prematurely.

"Often when you hear a gobble at 150 yards or so, and then everything goes silent for 10 or 15 minutes, the gobbler is cautiously coming in," he said. "That's when you want to be on full alert and listen for drumming or maybe wingtips dragging in the leaves. If you decide to move, it's a good idea to hit a locator call hard one time before doing so. That's just a bit of extra insurance to help avoid the misery of standing up, hearing a loud putt and seeing a longbeard run or fly off."

Another reason to relocate involves barriers — sometimes just figments of a gobbler's imagination — that can make a bird hang up. Really, many supposedly hung-up birds are with hens or in strut zones. However, even a love-starved gobbler that seems ready to find a hen can abruptly halt when he reaches a 2-foot-wide branch or a ditch he could easily hop across. Sometimes, however, a gobbler will fly a wide river or glide across a wide valley. You never know, but when a longbeard locks up, you must change positions.

Occasionally, selecting a setup involves a whim or, as Drury described it, "a feel that this might be a good place." On land you hunt regularly, strut zones always deserve attention. Just as a lunker largemouth or brown trout takes a prime holding spot after another fish is caught, a gobbler will replace another. Knowing the whereabouts of these areas can give you an advantage

WHEN YOU CONSCIOUSLY, consistently use sound tactics, success follows.

even if you don't hear a bird.

Along those lines, Harris uses another tactic.

"If I don't get on a bird, or if I have worked one or two without success, I start covering ground and maybe set up for a quarter- or half-hour in three or four spots," he said. "Eventually, I retrace my footsteps. Often, you will get a response as you backtrack. A turkey heard you the first time, but maybe he was with hens that left him, or maybe he just decided to investigate. Whatever the reason, I've had quite a bit of success doing this."

Knowing when and where to move, and linking your approach with a good setup, lies at the heart of turkey hunting. When you consciously, consistently use sound tactics, success follows. However, thoughtless, impetuous tactics — or, worse, no tactical planning — makes success unlikely. No general in his right mind would enter a battle without a carefully conceived strategy, and the mark of military genius is the ability to make tactical adjustments as an engagement unfolds.

That's just how it is with turkey hunting.

Working a Bird

Episodes from my first turkey season continue to haunt me. Thanks to the wisdom and generosity of my mentor, Parker Whedon, I killed a bird the first morning I hunted. My role that day was simple: hit man.

Yet from when I heard the tom gobble after we left our vehicle until he was flopping 25 yards away — not more than 30 minutes later — I became aware of some of the sport's endless subtleties and complexities.

I temporarily forgot those as we admired the bird and relived the moment, but a few words from Whedon brought me back to reality. I don't remember precisely what he said, but the gist was, "That's how it is done. Now you're on your own."

During the ensuing month, I learned much about how it wasn't done. I hunted every morning before rushing back to teach college classes, and then reversed the change from camouflage to coat and tie in the afternoon to try again. I frequently got toms to respond to my inept calling, but my twice-a-day outings soon became an ordeal. A turkey would respond to my calling or gobble on its own. I would close the distance and, many times, the bird would come in part of the way. Invariably, though, fate intervened. I got blindsided twice, picked an inopportune moment to answer another of nature's calls after a long period of silence, set up where no turkey would dare go, shot at a gobbler that was too far away, and in various other fashions fouled up the deal. Most of my myriad mistakes, however, derived from incompetence at knowing how to work a bird.

Through time, contemplation, study and advice from others, I managed to tip the balance a bit — at least to get an occasional turkey within range.

I suspect — other veteran hunters agree — that more turkeys are saved through inept calling or other actions connected with trying to lure in a gobbler. Even if that isn't true, you cannot deny the importance of possessing the skills to coax a longbeard within that magical 40-yard radius.

Having a two-way conversation with a gobbler is one of turkey hunting's delights. Hunters typically describe these conversations as "working a bird." Sometimes, of course, the befuddled, empty-handed hunter leaves the woods wondering whether he has done the working or has been worked over. Nonetheless, luring a bird within range epitomizes turkey hunting's excitement. It's challenging, captivating and, sometimes, rewarding.

Almost anything that can be said or written about working a bird is, to some degree, subjective. Every situation has nuances, and every gobbler has peculiarities. Still, some basic rules and commonality apply.

Knowing what type of call to use, when to call, how frequently to call, whether to call aggressively and when to keep things soft are important. Then there's the matter of mood, sometimes described as reading a bird or taking his temperature. In some situations, you might want to mimic a reluctant hen, but other situations demand conveying urgency.

There's no magical formula to lure in a gobbler. A technique that brings a lovesick 2-year-old at a trot, looking almost ridiculous as he tries to strut and hustle simultaneously, probably won't work with a long-spurred 4- to 5-year-old warrior. A method that works well at a lightly hunted private tract might send turkeys into a headlong retreat on hard-hunted public land. Tactics that work opening day will probably fail late in the season. In fact, things can change dramatically during a day.

In short, working a bird demands careful assessment and analysis. You must make decisions — some at a split-second — and implement your tactics quickly and confidently. If your first choice fails, you must go to Plan B. Experienced hunters exhibit quick thinking, decisiveness, adaptability and versatility.

Drury and Harris are among the best in the business. Their calling credentials are well established, and they possess the cumulative experience from thousands of gobbler encounters. They also possess a couple of intangibles. They innately know what it takes to tempt a tom. Even when they are wrong initially — they would admit that happens regularly — they probably have read the gobbler's book and switch to another tactic.

No matter what you call this positive state of mind — optimism, belief or self-assurance — it boils down to confidence. A confident hunter is capable, and he somehow establishes a link with his prey that attracts the bird. It

KNOWING WHAT TYPE of call to use, when to call, how frequently to call, whether to call aggressively and when to keep things soft are important.

ALTHOUGH HARRIS STRESSES calling techniques when working a bird, he also concentrates on getting close. "I'll use the terrain to get as close as is reasonable," he said, adding that close usually means no closer than 100 yards.

doesn't always happen, and no matter how skilled or confident you become, it won't always work. However, advice and suggestions from the Outland experts will make it more likely.

In Harris' view, the first thing to remember when calling a bird is that there's no set formula. However, he brings a specific philosophy to every setup.

"I want to take charge and do so right away," he said. "If you can get a turkey excited, I'm convinced he's more likely to come and more inclined to abandon some of his wariness. That's why I'm such a firm believer in the aggressive approach I use."

Drury also mentioned aggressiveness to bring a turkey close. His approach revolves around getting close.

"I'm constantly trying to penetrate his comfort zone," he said. "I'll push it to the limit in almost all circumstances, and I believe my overall success as a result of doing this far outweighs the occasional turkey I spook. If you want a phrase that sums up my thoughts, it would be, 'Close counts.'"

Although Harris stresses calling techniques when working a bird, he also concentrates on getting close.

"I'll use the terrain to get as close as is reasonable," he said, adding that close usually means no closer than 100 yards. "That's partly for safety, but that also leaves me some options when it comes to moving. I tend to err on the side of caution when it comes to closing ground on a gobbler, but there's no denying that there are some down sides to trying to work a bird from a long distance."

Drury frequently tries to get as close as 80 yards when he has a roosted bird pinpointed. Even during other conditions, he sometimes tries to get really tight.

"An example would be when a bird has stayed in place for some time but continues to gobble," he said. "That suggests there's a barrier or something else that makes him uncomfortable. Maybe I can slip or even crawl 15 or 20 yards, and that will make the difference."

Drury said the strongest argument for getting close is trying to ensure hens won't pick up the gobbler you're working.

"Even if it's possible to call a bird from hundreds of yards (I saw him do that in an open Colorado canyon), every extra yard increases the likelihood of him coming across an interested hen," he said. "If that happens, you can rest assured it's time to go hunt another turkey."

Anyone who has spent much time in turkey-rich territory, such as north-eastern Missouri, where hens sometimes cut you off at the pass several times in a morning, knows about this problem.

Drury and Harris agree that positioning is paramount.

"There's no doubt about it that it's easier to work a bird when you make it easy for him," Harris said. "Being close is a part of that, but you also need a set-up position where he feels safe and secure in approaching. That's one reason I look for strut zones, likely travel lanes and trail openings. These are places a gobbler is accustomed to using and is likely to approach."

Drury said that habitat preferences, particularly food sources, can dictate where a gobbler will want to go.

"Food sources are always changing," he said, "and if you pay attention to this and know what birds are eating, you can shift as they shift. A tom knows where hens are feeding on a daily basis, and if you try to work him from an unlikely location, it can add to the difficulty."

One of the most common problems in working a longbeard — it receives plenty of discussion among hunters — is dealing with hung-up turkeys. When you encounter a hung-up bird, Harris said, you must determine why the turkey isn't coming.

"If you can analyze the situation and get a good idea of what's holding the tom up, then you can address the problem," he said. "It's surprising how often doing nothing more than changing your location will do the trick. It isn't really normal for a hen to stay in one spot, yelping every so often, for 30 or 45 minutes."

Drury said the best time to relocate is immediately after a gobble.

"You know precisely where the bird is at that moment," he said, "whereas a move when you haven't heard a gobble for a few minutes might come just as the turkey has finally broken to come in."

Sometimes, you can't relocate. Then, Harris tries to create extra excitement.

"I'll use fighting purrs or the Wing Thing, throwing in some other sounds, to make it seem like a big fight," he said. "The idea is to pique the gobbler's curiosity."

He also offered this tip for hung-up birds.

"If a hung-up bird beats me, I'll ease off and try to find another turkey," he said. "But I'll come back to the spot later and try to figure out why the gobbler didn't come. Often, you can learn a lot by doing that."

"ONE GOOD TACTIC is double-teaming," Drury said. "I like to describe it as float-calling because one hunter stays put while the other moves directly away or laterally, calling as he goes."

Drury echoed Harris' comments about stimulating curiosity or interest with hung-up turkeys.

"One good tactic is double-teaming," he said. "I like to describe it as float-calling because one hunter stays put while the other moves directly away or laterally, calling as he goes."

This simulates a moving hen, which is natural and likely what a gobbler expects. Another of Drury's favored approaches for hung-up gobblers focuses on changing his calling style.

"I'll range from extremely aggressive to soft calling, or the reverse," he said. "Or you can sometimes make a turkey break just by throwing your calls."

This involves muffling boxes or slats, or turning your head if using a diaphragm, tube or wingbone.

Another way to work a hung-up bird involves a product Harris and Drury developed: the Spit 'n' Drum. This device mimics the sound of a strutting gobbler and serves as a quiet, low-key version of a fighting purr. It's designed to dupe a gobbler into believing another bird has intruded on its territory.

"A hung-up bird might not be willing to leave a spot just because he hears a hen yelping," Harris said. "If he thinks there's another gobbler displaying for that hen, he sometimes forgets all about holding his ground."

Drury believes the Spit 'n' Drum works especially well late in the season.

"It's also an excellent way to lure a boss tom," he said. "Those older, wiser birds are naturally more reluctant, and I think a lot of the turkeys we describe as hanging up are actually just ones that are especially wary. They lose some of that wariness when they hear what they think is the sound of another gobbler."

Familiarity with a bird might also dictate how it should be worked.

"I like to get a history on a bird when I can," Harris said. "When high-profile hunters like Mark or me visit a particular place, the local hunters always want us to deal with the bad bird."

Drury agreed.

"I don't want the turkey that has whipped all the hunters around and heard all sorts of calling," he said. "Just give me a lonely 2-year-old."

Still, Drury and Harris have plenty of experience with difficult turkeys and acknowledge such birds require special treatment.

"I've learned — mostly the hard way — that sometimes the best thing you can do is to leave a won't-come bird for another day," Drury said. "You don't want to burn your chip or waste all your hunting time on a turkey that clearly won't come. Sometimes, the most sensible thing to do is leave a bird that won't work and find one that will."

Harris said when you encounter an especially difficult turkey, it might be wise to try somewhere else. However, if a tough bird is the only game in town, you might try some other tactics. Harris adjusts when circumstances dictate.

"Maybe you just want to slip in close and play the cautious waiting game," he said. "I find this particularly effective later in the season as birds become warier and less vocal because of hunting pressure."

In these conditions, Harris likes to use his "scared-hen" ploy.

"I keep my calling really soft and subdued," he said, "and just cluck and purr after I've gotten really tight. This is when you need those qualities of woodsmanship to be at their best. The increased foliage normally present later in the season will help you some, and I make a point of avoiding human travel zones. Get off the trails and ridgelines, and take it nice and slow, being as quiet as possible. Also, remember that your turkey is likely to come sneaking in without making a sound."

If you experience that infrequent situation when more than one gobbling turkey might work, Drury offered this advice.

"Any time you can get between two gobbling turkeys, especially if you can get them playing off one another, you're in an ideal situation," he said.

Drury has also learned that birds roosted at elevated locations — ridge lines and bluffs, for example — tend to be more likely to come to calling than those roosted in low areas such as river bottoms or next to fields.

"My theory is that birds that are lower are more likely to be with hens, but those up high want the additional altitude to help them look for and hear hens," he said. "Certainly, I've found that my overall ratio of success in calling in gobblers is better with high-up birds."

Finally, remember that when it comes to working a bird, you can't punch a clock.

"You have to get in a turkey mode, not a human mode," Drury said. Harris recalled the phrase "on turkey time." That is, time means nothing to a turkey, so it should mean nothing to you.

"Always give a turkey time to work," Drury said. "Listen, listen, listen, and then listen some more."

Harris agreed.

"Patience should be a turkey hunter's closest friend when he is working a gobbler," he said.

Closing the Deal

It doesn't matter whether a gobbler comes like he was on a string, or if he plays a coy waiting game that leaves you a bundle of nerves addled by an adrenaline overdose. When enough things fall into place, the moment of truth arrives. This occurs when you make the irrevocable decision to pull the trigger. It can be magic — or tragic.

Once in a blue moon, fate might intervene. A gobbler might peck at a grasshopper at the most inopportune moment, or a previously undetected hole in your gun's pattern could leave the bird unscathed. Those rare occasions aside, closing the sale depends on the hunter.

Celebration after a clean kill might be bittersweet, but a miss brings pure misery. You relive misses — not once, but again and again. In my book, anyone who claims he has never missed a turkey has unwittingly revealed one of two things: He is a shameless scoundrel who plays fast and loose with the truth — the sort of scamp who might abscond with the church treasury — or he simply hasn't shot at a lot of turkeys.

"Everyone misses turkeys," Drury said. "And a miss is nothing to be ashamed of. Misses happen."

That's a fact of turkey hunting life. However, you want to minimize your misses.

Like many other aspects of the sport, preparation and patience are critical. You must go through the procedures — patterning, choosing the best load, learning to judge distances — that give you confidence in your gun when the moment of truth arrives.

Of course, it's not just the gun that must perform. A gun is merely a tool, albeit a highly engineered, supremely efficient one. The ultimate performance test rests with you. Turkey hunting is a major test of your sporting mettle, because you must handle matters efficiently in pressure-packed situations when countless things can — and do — go wrong. Surely, Mr. Murphy of Murphy's Law was a turkey hunter. Somehow, you must display the strength of character, steely nerves and steady hand to wait out a gobbler when the shot is at hand. The meaning of "turkey time" becomes clear as minute follows agonizing minute when you wait for a bird to cover those final few yards.

When it comes to preparation, suffice to say, overdoing matters is almost impossible. After all, the precursors of that make-or-break moment likely include pre-season scouting, countless hours of calling practice, and perhaps the better part of a lifetime spent gradually acquiring the skills and wisdom we call woodscraft.

More immediately, you have located a bird, worked him within range and chosen the time and place for the shot. However, these factors, the cumulative preparation of days, months or possibly years, can crash down like a house of cards with that most malevolent miscue — a miss.

"What you don't ever want to happen is a miss that could easily have been avoided," Drury said. "As is true with so many aspects of the sport, the solution to most misses lies with doing everything possible to ensure readiness when that magic moment arrives."

Harris shook his head in mock dismay when the subject of misses was broached.

"I've missed turkeys," he said, and then turned to me with a grin and added, "and you've missed turkeys."

Harris believes misses come with the sport and are part of every hunter's lot.

"Still, any hunter worth his salt will take every precaution to avoid missing," he said. "You owe it not only to yourself but to the turkey."

When it comes to misses, Harris and Drury offered several recommendations — a training regimen, if you will — for serious hunters. They fall into several categories, each of which deserves examination. By following their program, you should be ready when that exciting, exacting second arrives when it's time to, as guides often whisper, "take him."

KNOW AND TRUST YOUR GUN

"I believe having a gun you're intimately familiar with is quite important," Drury said. "You don't need to be fumbling for a safety that isn't where you reached, or loading in the darkness when you aren't exactly sure how the receiver works. To attain that familiarity, get plenty of use from your gun before you take to the woods."

You can do this through patterning, and some hunters — especially those with a multipurpose shotgun — gain familiarity through other shooting, such as sporting clays or maybe even dove hunting. After all, even shotguns designed for turkey hunting typically come with various chokes, and all but the shortest barrels work reasonably well for wing-shooting. Certainly, the frequent mounting, pushing off the safety and firing associated with shooting clay birds provides familiarity.

In Harris' view, nothing beats a patterning board for understanding a gun.

"It's always a good idea," he said, "even with an old reliable gun you've used for years, to fire a few rounds at a turkey pattern. For example, when I travel to hunt, I make a point of trying to do that after I arrive. I don't shoot a scoped shotgun, but it still reassures me that everything is functioning and in order. Obviously, for those who do prefer a shotgun with a scope, this is essential.

"A few shots at a turkey pattern and studying the results renews your confidence, and I believe having faith in your firearm can make a difference. Certainly, you don't want to be hunting with an unproven gun or one in which you have less than absolute faith. Turkey hunting has enough built-in uncertainties without adding to them."

Drury also advocates patterning and said you should always fine-tune any new element.

"Whether it's a new gun, a new choke or a new shotshell, it's vital to know precisely how it performs," he said. "Patterning will address all aspects of newness, except how well a load penetrates."

Drury and Harris approach their preparations in similar fashion.

"Any time I try out a new gun, I begin by inserting the appropriate M.A.D. Max choke tube," he said. "After that's done, I like to try various shot sizes and loads to see which patterns best."

DISCERNING DISTANCE

Although peeking up from the stock likely accounts for most misses, misjudging distance causes its share. At least misses that result from peeking are clean, because the pattern typically flies over a turkey's head. However, when you think a turkey is closer than it is, the result is often a wounded bird. That is ample reason to firmly understand distance.

Guns vary somewhat in their effective killing range, and factors such as shot size, choke constriction, powder load, barrel length, shot penetration and others affect how far you should shoot. However, you must determine these long before you look down a gun barrel at a turkey.

Individual guns might be exceptions, but here are some general distances for maximum killing ranges using optimum loads:

10-gauge: 45 to 50 yards

12-gauge: 40 to 45 yards

16-gauge: 35 to 40 yards

20-gauge: 30 to 35 yards

.410-gauge: 25 yards or less

Sure, you regularly hear hunters brag about 60-yard shots or a flat-out-deadly gun that never fails at 55 yards. Anyone who makes such statements should be ashamed, because they're admitting they have less than proper respect for turkeys. Those are crippling ranges, not killing distances, although turkeys can undeniably be killed at such extended ranges.

"Can be" is not good enough. When you shoot, a turkey should be sufficiently close so an accurate shot will kill him.

Much of distance judgment depends on woodsmanship. In the woods, make a point of constantly looking at a tree, stump or other object and estimating how far it is. That can add fun to pre-season scouting rambles or any walk in the woods. Only when you can judge 40 yards consistently, with no more than two or three yards error, are you ready. Even then, that might not be enough. For most hunters, a turkey in a field or woods with a sparse understory looks closer than it is. The temptation to take a long shot can be strong.

"One way of taking care of judging distance is picking out landmarks within your range of fire that you know are close enough for you to kill a turkey," Harris said. "Then you can say to yourself, 'If he passes that tree, I can kill him.'"

You can step off that distance to be certain, provided an approaching gobbler isn't right on top of you.

Harris said decoys can also help you deal with distance.

"I like to put my decoys out about 25 or 30 yards from where I set up," he said. "That means any turkey that comes to them will be well within range. Just make sure they aren't too close, because a really tight shot is difficult.

MUCH OF DISTANCE JUDGMENT depends on woodsmanship. In the woods, make a point of constantly looking at a tree, stump or other object and estimating how far it is.

Your pattern has no chance to open up. Also, there are safety considerations, and a bird coming from an unexpected direction could be quite close to you and the decoys before you see him. He's more likely to bust you then."

If you have difficulty judging distance, technology can provide a simple solution. If you still cannot accurately judge distance after repeated efforts, a rangefinder or some types of turkey scopes might be the answer. With a rangefinder, you can, as mentioned previously, pick out nearby landmarks to define your kill zone and be prepared when a tom shows up. Also, some scopes are designed to indicate a turkey is in range — usually 40 yards — when you see all of a bird's body or its neck when extended. These tools add complexity, but show me a turkey hunter who isn't nuts about gadgets and accessories, and I'll show you a rare soul.

PROPER POSITIONING

Turkey hunters constantly bemoan the common occurrence of being "wrong-sided" by a gobbler. This happens when a turkey — the bird you're working or another tom — shows up away from where you have your gun pointed. No matter how flexible you are, even your best contortionist imita-

"EXPERIENCE HAS TAUGHT ME that when a tom takes a circular route coming in, you have to be willing to commit to dramatic repositioning when circumstances dictate," said Drury. "If that means scooting halfway around the base of a tree in a hurry, you've just got to do it."

tion won't allow more than 120 to 130 degrees of gun movement while seated. That is, more than half of a turkey's possible approach angles will be where you cannot point, much less take a careful shot, without repositioning.

You should do everything possible to ensure that when a gobbler appears, it will be within your range of gun swing. Ideally, swing won't even be involved. In a perfect situation, when the turkey reaches the point where you want to shoot, it will be directly where your gun barrel was pointed all along.

The Outland experts have much to say about this issue. That's revealing because it suggests positioning for a shot deserves more attention than it receives.

"Have the gun pointed where the gobbler is going, not where he is when you hear him," Drury said. "Then, while the bird works toward you, make minor adjustments as needed so long as the gobbler remains out of sight. Also, experience has taught me that when a tom takes a circular route coming in, you have to be willing to commit to dramatic repositioning when circumstances dictate. If that means scooting halfway around the base of a tree in a hurry, you've just got to do it."

Harris offered several specific tips.

"I try to set up so that my left shoulder is in the direction from where I expect the bird to come," he said. "It's easy for someone who shoots right-handed like me to move the gun to the left, but if your right shoulder is pointing toward where you expect the bird, you have almost no room for error farther right."

Try resting a gun barrel on your right knee and swinging farther to the right, and you will see what Harris means.

"Then, get the gun into a position you are comfortable with and that's well supported," he said. "The wait could be long, and no matter how strong you are, holding a gun rock steady without support cannot be done for extended periods of time."

For Harris, an ideal support position can be maintained for a half-hour or longer, if needed.

"I like to lock my left forearm on my left thigh," he said. "It gives me a good, solid, comfortable brace."

Harris said it's not essential to have your gun shouldered continuously when a bird seems close. Barrel direction, however, is vital.

"You want to have your barrel pointed in the general direction of the turkey even if it is not up," he said. "Easing a gun up to your shoulder and lowering your cheek to the stock involves far less movement than having to move the gun up and swing it."

He also cautioned against getting into and shooting from awkward positions.

"If you tilt your gun barrel, you change your sight plane," he said. "That greatly increases the likelihood of a miss."

"You really shouldn't take an awkward shot," Drury said. "For example, if you've swung as far right as you can, like when a bird comes in from the right and behind you, chances are even the few pounds of pressure needed to squeeze the trigger will pull you to the left enough to lead to a miss."

Obviously, this is when patience comes into play. Wait the bird out. Maybe it will drift into better position, or perhaps it will go behind a tree or other cover, letting you make a quick readjustment.

Harris and Drury said decoys can be a major aid for shot positioning. Unless something spooks a gobbler, he'll likely move in to investigate the fakes. If you've positioned yourself appropriately in relation to the decoys, you should be rewarded with a good shot.

Harris also offered some personal advice on positioning.

"If you work at it and practice, the ability to shoot left-handed or right-handed can be a distinct advantage," he said. "After all, it doubles the area you can cover. But I don't recommend doing this unless you have confidence in your ability to change shoulders and have done it a lot. One of the first times I tried this, it was without having really studied shooting left-handed or practicing it much. I killed the turkey but almost broke my nose in the process."

EXECUTING THE SHOT AND ITS AFTERMATH

"When the moment for taking the shot arrives, you want to make the gobbler get his head up," Harris said. "Putting or giving a hard cluck will usually work, but you want to be certain the bird is within range and not where it could mean a difficult or partly obstructed shot if he goes on alert."

Harris' thinking is straightforward. When a gobbler extends its neck, it offers the largest possible kill area.

Drury's advice follows similar lines.

"Usually, a sharp cluck will do the trick," he said. "but not always. Sometimes, a tom gets so absorbed in strutting, especially when you're using decoys, that even a cluck won't work. At such times, I'll increase the volume quite a bit. Do whatever it takes to get the bird to raise its head, and if possible, you want him standing still. After all, you're almost shooting a rifle at close range, and it's much easier to hit a stationary target."

Sometimes, of course, a gobbler decides something is wrong before the hunter believes everything is right. If that happens, and a gobbler is putting and starting to walk away, Harris has a suggestion.

"If a turkey putts, I'll call to him," he said. "It might slow him down or stop him for a moment, and his head will almost certainly go up. Then there's a chance for a shot."

Even if that doesn't work, you have nothing to lose. The turkey, for whatever reason, has already seen enough and decided the game is up. If it putts, sharply adjusts its wings or turns to walk away, that indicates the bird is leaving.

"Before I make this final call, I already have the safety off, the gun mounted and the bead on the bird," Harris said.

You don't want to push off the safety too quickly. A good rule of thumb is to do this when you first see the gobbler. However, that might not be appropriate with a field turkey because the bird is likely far away. Push off the safety with little movement and as quietly as possible. Even the seemingly unobtrusive click of a carelessly pushed safety can spook a gobbler.

Similarly, mounting or moving the gun into position should be done when the bird is out of sight, or so slowly it's almost imperceptible. Too often, the opposite happens.

"Trying to get the gun up and on the turkey after he's already in range costs hunters a lot of turkeys," Drury said. "Make a point of moving your eyes, not your head, when watching or looking for an incoming turkey. Even the best of camouflage doesn't hide movement. If you have to move your head or gun when the bird is visible, do it slower than slow."

Harris said some planning can help avoid problems with moving.

"Find opportunities to make the last, slight and final adjustment to the gun," he said. "You might use a tree as the tom passes behind it, wait until he fans and pirouettes, or move a bit when he gobbles. Whatever you do, you want to avoid a sudden, snap movement. If I'm caught unprepared, I'll usually let the bird walk away, and then maybe I can work him back in again. On the other hand, if you spook a gobbler, it's unlikely you will get the bird back within range.

"Hunter movement has been the salvation of many longbeards, but the most common mistake connected with preparing for and executing the shot is failure to get down on the stock. It's so easy to be intrigued with what's going on, and you watch it with your head far too high."

Often, you put the bead on the target but don't look straight down the barrel. One partial solution is to use a gun with two beads. In addition, consider the old wing-shooter's adage: Wood (the hunter's cheek) to wood (the stock).

"Also, remember you're shooting the gun as if it is a rifle, not a shotgun," Harris said.

Drury agreed.

"Aim, don't just shoot," he said. "You've got to control your nerves. That's easy enough to say, but the word 'hyperventilate' is commonly used in hunting tales."

Sometimes, it helps to remind yourself it's just a turkey.

"A few deep breaths often help, and much like a basketball player taking a free throw, you need to have good breath control," Drury said. "After you're steady and ready, a slow, calm trigger squeeze is what you want."

Like an expert bench-shooter, a turkey hunter should never know exactly when the gun will fire. That's worth remembering, because it's a far cry from typical wing-shooting.

After you shoot, it's natural to want to release the wellspring of emotions that have built up during the hunt. Perhaps that's why conventional turkey hunting wisdom suggests you scramble to your feet and rush to, hopefully, a flopping gobbler. The idea is to get your feet or hands on the bird's neck quickly, guaranteeing it won't get back up and get away.

During some circumstances, that might be logical. For example, if you are hunting with a muzzleloader, it's a one-shot deal, and it makes sense to burst through the cloud of smoke doing your best imitation of a fullback. Similarly, if you're anxious about keeping a turkey in good shape for photography or the taxidermist, you want to minimize damage. This means preventing excess flopping and resultant feather loss, or stopping a bird from getting wet in dew-drenched grass, which detracts from its appearance.

However, it's sometimes wise for you to remain in place and alert.

"You want to make sure he's anchored," Drury said. "If not, be ready to follow up with a second shot."

A second shot will likely be more accurate if taken from a settled, ready

"YOU NEED TO SAVOR the moment then," Mark Drury said. "No matter how many times you relive it in your mind in the months and years to come, nothing quite matches those treasured moments when you're there with your turkey. Then, all is truly right in the hunter's world."

IF YOU'RE ANXIOUS ABOUT KEEPING a turkey in good shape for photography or the taxidermist, you want to minimize damage. This means preventing excess flopping and resultant feather loss, or stopping a bird from getting wet in dew-drenched grass, which detracts from its appearance.

position rather than during a mad scramble. If you're shooting a pump, recycling the gun immediately after the shot should be reflexive. Regardless of your gun, keep the barrel pointed toward the bird and ready.

Harris also offered another consideration.

"Push the safety back in place before getting up," he said. "You don't want to be running — or even walking — with a gun that is ready to fire."

However, never set the gun down at your setup and go to the bird.

"By all means, carry the gun with you as you approach the bird," Harris said. "That way, if the bird shows signs of getting up, you can take another shot. Incidentally, one of the surest signs a bird isn't completely finished is a raised neck. If a bird puts his head back up or gets back to his feet, another shot is in order."

Also, avoid being spurred by downed birds.

"Let him get his flopping out," Drury said. "Take a look at the damage turkeys sometime show from fighting, and you'll see what I mean. A sharp-spurred tom with some real kick left in him can tear your arms or hands up in a hurry."

No matter what you do after the shot, Harris and Drury said, it's important to react properly to a kill.

"It's a special time," Harris said. "After the high-fiving and hollering are finished when I'm hunting with someone else, I always take a few moments of reflection."

He said a kill strikes him more meaningfully when hunting alone.

"The solitude gives me the opportunity to think about things in my own way and at my own pace," he said. "When I'm kneeling and admiring a beard or spurs, there's a sort of real reverence involved."

Drury said every turkey is truly special.

"You need to savor the moment then," he said. "No matter how many times you relive it in your mind in the months and years to come, nothing quite matches those treasured moments when you're there with your turkey. Then, all is truly right in the hunter's world."

Drury said that when we shared a hunt in Colorado. Almost immediately after his comment, distant thunder startled a tom into gobbling. That was a special moment, and hopefully the Outland experts' suggestions will bring similar magical days to your hunting.

Section 4
The Ethos of the Hunt

Daniel E. Schmidt

Safety and Ethics

SAFETY

Any detailed examination of turkey hunting must address safety. The sport's nature — how and where turkeys are hunted, and its up-close-and-personal methods — means safety should be paramount.

Too often, the quest for a turkey can assume a competitive aspect that's unsafe and, at least arguably, unethical. The only true competition should be between the hunter and his quarry, not with fellow hunters. However, a common scenario sees a hunter, perhaps part of a club or someone who shares news with friends, become increasingly desperate to kill a gobbler as one birdless day succeeds another.

He listens to glowing reports about chess matches with gobblers, which end with a fine bird being carried from the field. As these stories mount, he begins to feel desperation. He is so anxious to kill a tom and match his buddies' exploits he sets the stage for a tragic mistake.

If you think otherwise, ask yourself some questions. Have you mistaken an object — inanimate or animate — for a gobbler? Honesty will likely compel you to admit that, at some point, a cardinal, the tip of a budding buckeye or a strangely shaped limb has tricked you into thinking you were looking at a turkey's wattles. Or have you thought noise — maybe a squirrel rustling in dry leaves or a hunter walking through the woods — was an approaching tom? I'm guilty on both counts, and the same holds true with most turkey hunters.

However, being fooled by sights or sounds need not translate to foolishness. That's where anxiety, desperation or an overbearing desire to score can lead to shooting at something you really can't see. Also, considering the widespread use of decoys, full camouflage and turkey vocalizations, you have ample justification for constant safety consciousness. Although significant in any type of hunting, safety awareness is probably more important for turkey hunters.

Generations ago, when the average American lived close to the land in a rural area, proper gun handling and awareness of hunting and firearms safety were integral in many youngsters' upbringings. What's now called hunter-safety training was provided by fathers, grandfathers, uncles or other adult mentors, and it occurred in the classroom of the wild through many years rather than during a one- or two-day session held primarily indoors. There is little question about which approach produced safer hunters. Sadly, these once-common adolescent apprenticeships belong to a world we have largely lost.

Nowadays, most youngsters don't enjoy the privilege of growing up with the timeless tutelage I knew as a boy, or that's detailed in Robert Ruark's enduring *The Old Man and the Boy*. Likewise, many modern turkey hunters started the sport as adults. It's not their fault, but they missed the education afforded by a gradual induction — through several building blocks, by learning one lesson after another — into turkey hunting's joys.

As adults, many folks understandably — though often erroneously — believe they're qualified to hunt and are totally responsible. Some are, but many aren't.

Generally, everyone — no matter their background in safety training and awareness — should stay aware of the Ten Commandments of Safety.

These guidelines constitute the proper beginning, no matter your experience, and remain vital every time you pick up a gun. The commandments should be second nature, implanted in your mind. They should never be forgotten. For reinforcement, and as an introduction to the Outland experts' thoughts about safety, let's review them.

➤ Always keep your gun's muzzle pointed in a safe direction. This is the basic, essential rule upon which all gun safety is built. If a muzzle were never pointed at anything except intended targets, accidents wouldn't happen. For turkey hunters, this typically comes into play when hunting with partners and moving. Control your muzzle at all times.

➤ Firearms should be unloaded when not in use. The ramifications are obvious.

Always unload your gun before getting into a vehicle, when crossing a

Brian Lovett

GENERALLY, EVERYONE — no matter their background in safety training and awareness — should stay aware of the Ten Commandments of Safety. These guidelines remain vital every time you pick up a gun.

fence or similar obstacle and in any potentially perilous situation. When hunting with a youngster or beginner, it's wise to wait until you set up before loading.

➤ Don't rely on your gun's safety. Treat any gun as if it could fire at any time. That means keeping your finger away from the trigger until you are ready to shoot. Similarly, avoid the nervous habit of repeatedly clicking a safety on and off. That's dangerous and could scare off an unseen tom. Slip the safety off when you see a gobbler or when a turkey gobbles nearby. After the shot, don't forget to push the safety back on before running to your bird.

➤ Be sure of your target and beyond. An unthinking hunter might argue that he need not worry about anything but his target because a shotgun's killing range is limited. However, keen awareness of the target and what's behind it is a must. Otherwise, you might shoot one bird and learn others were behind it. Similarly, during low light or in areas with high hunting pressure, you must be sure you're shooting at a gobbler, not a hen. If in doubt — never mind that a gobble just emanated from where you saw movement — don't shoot.

ALWAYS REMEMBER to do the right thing safety-wise when crossing fences, climbing rock walls or otherwise getting in a position where a slip-up could happen.The best thing to do is unload and then reload after negotiating the obstacle.

➤ Use the correct ammunition. This might seem obvious and scarcely worth mention, but mistakes such as cramming a 20-gauge shell into a 12-gauge chamber could result in tragedy.

Also, although this section deals with safety instead of ethics, no turkey hunter wants to mistakenly place a pigeon load with a minimal powder charge and No. 8 shot in his gun. It will likely result in a crippled bird and a lost opportunity.

➤ If your gun doesn't fire when you pull the trigger, handle it with care. Be keenly aware of your muzzle direction, and keep your face away from the breech.

If you're using a modern gun, carefully open the breech, and extract the shell. If you're using a muzzleloader, remember that you could be experiencing a slow-fire. If that's the case — and the gobbler hasn't spooked — continue holding on him for several seconds.

➤ Always wear eye and ear protection when shooting. This doesn't relate to turkey hunting in a major way, although hearing enhancements have become popular for turkey hunters, and many manufacturers also offer hearing protection. One argument for wearing shooting glasses is that they protect your eyes from twigs and limbs while moving through the woods. Anyone who has been smacked in the eye by a limb accidentally released by a buddy knows how painful and potentially dangerous this can be.

➤ Be sure the barrel is clear of obstructions before shooting. This is basic. For guns that break down — double-barrels and over-and-unders — you can easily do this by looking down the barrels — always from the breech end — before loading. For pumps and autoloaders, open the action, and look through the barrel. It's also wise, for safety and your gun's longevity, to clean the bore and outside of the gun after every trip afield. Even if you don't shoot, moisture and dirt accumulation can have damaging and perhaps dangerous effects.

➤ Don't alter or modify your gun, and have guns serviced regularly. Unless you're a qualified gunsmith or have a detailed knowledge of gun repair, leave changes to experts.

Specialized turkey guns might not see much service in terms of shots taken, but many hunters use multipurpose shotguns. No matter how well these are made, they won't last forever, and occasional servicing might be required. Also, remember that turkey loads pack a punch, and this affects a gun. If something seems loose or isn't working correctly, don't take a chance.

➤ Learn the mechanical and handling characteristics of your firearm. This is a must. You don't want to be fumbling for a thumb safety when it's located on the trigger guard, or looking for a barrel selector when a gun has two triggers. For those who use gun accessories, such as the increasingly popular red-dot scopes, remember to turn these on and off. Familiarity with your gun results in a safer and likely more successful hunt. Learn your gun's characteristics at the firing range or patterning board — not while hunting.

As you might expect, given their early introduction to turkey hunting, Drury and Harris learned safety principles early on.

"When it comes to safety, you start with the obvious — follow all the basic rules," Drury said.

Drury also added several specific suggestions for safe gun handling.

"It's a good idea to consider waiting until you set up before loading your gun," he said. "That removes the problem of walking with a loaded shotgun, and incidentally takes away the temptation for a sudden shot at a bird you might not have identified as a gobbler.

"It also removes the possibility of crippling a tom with a rushed or unwise shot. In other words, keep the gun unfireable until you're completely ready to fire."

Drury also stressed muzzle direction.

"I always watch how someone handles his gun the first time I'm afield with him," he said. "If a hunter displays any carelessness or lets his muzzle stray, I'll say something."

Drury believes the increased awareness from such comments outweighs any awkwardness that might result. He suggested hunters take such steps if they encounter similar situations.

"Two other areas connected with gun handling also deserve careful attention," he said. "One is invariably mentioned in any basic coverage of safety but the second seldom receives notice. Always remember to do the right thing safety-wise when crossing fences, climbing rock walls or otherwise getting in a position where a slip-up could happen. In these situations, the best thing to do is unload and then reload after negotiating the obstacle. Or, when with a companion, hold his gun until he crosses, and then have him do the same while you cross."

The second situation — one that's often overlooked — occurs after someone kills a gobbler. It's easy to forget to put the safety back on, which can make common post-kill situations — such as exchanging high-fives or a mad

30- to 40-yard rush to a flopping longbeard — dangerous.

In these circumstances, do one of two things. If you rush to a turkey immediately after firing — most longtime hunters advocate this — make sure to push the safety back on before you tear off to the tom. Otherwise, stay in place, and remain ready for a second shot, if needed.

"You will be more likely to make a good shot this way than while in the midst of a 50-yard dash after a crippled and fleeing bird," Drury said.

Harris also urged caution after a shot.

"Running to a dead or dying bird with the safety off can be a problem, and I've seen it happen more than once," he said. "I believe in getting to the tom quickly, but before doing that, you must push the safety back. In fact, most of the time when I'm hunting with someone else, I make a point of asking him about the safety. This shouldn't offend anyone, because you can never place too much emphasis on being safe."

Harris also believes in defensive hunting. To him, one of the critical elements is remaining aware of potential dangers posed by other hunters.

"If I hear a hen, I immediately ask myself, 'Could that be a hunter?'" he said.

Harris avoids what he calls "precarious situations." He said no sensible sportsman will "crowd an area with another hunter present. If you find someone else is hunting — and particularly if he's working a bird — just back off. That's not only wise from a safety standpoint. It's sound sporting ethics."

Drury also addressed the issue.

"My rule of thumb in such situations is simple," he said. "If a guy is working a bird, it's his. In fact, if someone starts competing with me on a tom I started working first, it's still his. I just go find another turkey. There's always a gobbling turkey somewhere else, and neither danger nor a potential confrontation is worth it."

Harris believes chance encounters with other hunters can pose real danger. He follows several rules when he hears or sees other hunters or suspects they might be present.

"If you see someone, vocalize right away," he said. "Do this in a clear, audible voice, but don't yell or do something that could frighten someone. Never make sudden motions, such as waving your arm or hat. A guy with jumpy nerves and an itchy trigger finger could unthinkingly fire at movement."

Brian Lovett

When carrying decoys afield, make sure they're covered. Don't even let a decoy's head poke out of your vest, and avoid carrying them under your arm or in the open.

When Harris senses another hunter could be in the area — when he hears hen yelps that don't sound true, for example — he blows "shave and a haircut, two bits" on a crow call.

"That sort of thing can also be useful when you have a buddy hunting in the same area," he said. "You might even want to have some sort of pre-arranged vocal signal to alert one another to your whereabouts."

Decoys and dead turkeys constitute further safety concerns. When using decoys, Harris said, make sure you can see for a long distance.

"Although this might mean you're a bit more exposed to a turkey's excellent vision, good camouflage and the fact that the decoys should be a bird's focal point work in your favor," he said.

Harris also suggested "covering your rear" when using decoys, which typically means setting up against a tree wider than your body, or a similarly safe site such as a solid tree lap, a stone fence, steep bluffs or large boulders.

When carrying decoys afield, Harris said, make sure they're covered. Don't even let a decoy's head poke out of your vest, and avoid carrying them under your arm or in the open. It takes extra time to correctly store decoys in a vest or a fluorescent orange bag, but it's worthwhile. With a vest, take it off and place the decoys inside, or have a fellow hunter make sure decoys are out of sight.

"You certainly don't want to give anyone so much as a glimpse of something that looks like a turkey," Harris said.

Beyond these pointers, Drury and Harris reminded hunters that safety always involves awareness and common sense. Likewise, hunters should be ready, if the situation arises, to point out unsafe behavior. In factories and machine shops of yesteryear, signs reading "Think Safety" and "Safety First" adorned walls and doorways. Similar notices should probably be as ubiquitous as posted signs in today's hunting world. Because they aren't, it's the responsibility of every hunter to remember that message.

ETHICS

As I've suggested, an ethical hunter should constantly be aware of safety. Most hunters, if pressed, could provide many other characteristics associated with scrupulous, conscientious and proper behavior. However, producing a cogent definition of hunting ethics can be daunting. This, at least in part, is because ethics are intensely personal. A message my father constantly imparted during my sporting apprenticeship, although not a definition, goes to the heart of the issue.

"The measure of a hunter's ethics," Dad said repeatedly, "is what he does when no one is watching."

What he was suggesting — rightly so — was that the ultimate definition of ethics comes from within. It varies from one hunter to another, yet there is common ground with which no honest, well-intentioned hunter could disagree. Or, as is often said, hunting has two types of laws: written ones enforceable by law and unwritten ones involving a code of honor.

Some matters are obvious, such as rigid adherence to regulations covering seasons, weapons, licenses, bag limits, hunting hours and the like. However, obeying laws constitutes little more than a starting point. After all, laws don't cover many — if any — of the matters described as fair chase. Here's a capsule of some critical aspects of fair chase for turkey hunting.

➤ Avoid taking long shots. Know your gun and its potential, and select shots accordingly. Taking a 60-yard shot, hoping a stray pellet or two will hit a vital spot, will likely cripple a longbeard rather than kill it.

➤ If any shot — no matter how selective — wounds a turkey, make unstinting efforts to find and retrieve the bird.

➤ Respect your quarry. Use the bird as fully as possible — as table fare, treasured mementos, to make wingbone calls or to fletch arrows. Clean your bird quickly, and dispose of remains properly. Many hunters go further and pause for a moment of reflection when they kill a turkey. For most, the moment is bittersweet.

➤ Hone your hunting skills to the sharpest. This gives you greater chances of success and fuller appreciation of the turkey's habits and habitat.

Along with pursuing the tenets of fair chase, an ethical hunter should be an advocate for the resource and an ambassador for the sport. You can accomplish this many ways, but all involve giving. Those gifts might be monetary. More often, however, they involve willingness to give your spare time and share the sport with others. You might do this by serving as a mentor to a youngster or new turkey hunter. Or, you might be an unofficial guide to a friend or landowner who lets you hunt. Be a giver, not a taker.

Membership in conservation organizations — notably the National Wild Turkey Federation — provides financial assistance for habitat improvement, research and restoration. However, meaningful membership involves more than paying dues. It means helping with fund-raisers, working on habitat projects, helping at shows or calling contests, and exhibiting a willingness to go the extra mile. An ethical hunter cares, and he shares.

Activism and awareness also come under the umbrella of ethics. Concerned hunters are citizens who participate. They study voting records of local and national officials and make studied judgments on issues. It's troubling to learn, according to surveys, that hunting-license holders are not among the most active voters. Despite the efforts of groups such as the National Rifle Association and the Wildlife Legislative Fund of America to foster knowledge of hunting and gun-rights developments, too many hunters seem unaware of the threats to America's rich, proud hunting heritage. An ethical hunter is an informed, active citizen. He can speak convincingly about the long-term benefits of the Pittman-Robertson Act, and how hunters have paid for wildlife protection, habitat acquisition and other conservation efforts. He understands the close relationship between hunting and wildlife management, appreciates the lessons of hunting's past, and keeps a keen eye on the future. In short, he is an effective, eloquent spokesman for hunting, whether he communicates through words or deeds.

You've likely shaken your head when watching or reading about the outrageous, often illegal deeds of anti-hunters. However, have you done anything to counter their efforts? Does your hunting club participate in a litter pick-up program, such as Adopt-a-Highway? Have you contributed to Hunters for the Hungry or similar groups that help feed the impoverished? Have you volunteered with youth programs or National Hunting and Fishing Day activities in your area? Have you offered to share your expertise with Becoming an Outdoorswoman or Women in the Outdoors programs? Hopefully, you can answer "yes" to one or more of these questions. Too often, good intentions fall short of positive actions. An ethical hunter thinks about these things and does his part — maybe more.

Another aspect of ethics must be mentioned. This is the relationship between hunters and landowners. An ethical hunter always treats the land on which he hunts — whether private or public — as his own. The Golden Rule should be your guide.

Never litter. Better yet, pick up litter others have left. Heed posted signs, close gates and use roads, especially if the weather has been wet and travel could cause damage. Remember some wisdom my grandfather shared: "Thank you doesn't cost anything, but it will buy you a lot."

Harris got to the heart of ethics when he said, "We all have to work to keep the sport strong. One of the best ways to do this is through image. All

Daniel E. Schmidt

AN ETHICAL HUNTER always treats the land on which he hunts — whether private or public — as his own. The Golden Rule should be your guide.

of us need to work — and work hard — to counter image-related problems. Be proud of our country's hunting heritage, and give others reason to be proud as well."

Harris offered an example of how he tries to project a positive image.

"When I travel, I make a practice of wearing camouflage clothing," he said. "My attire is clean and neatly pressed, and it says to others, 'He's a hunter.'"

By doing this and demonstrating courtesy in public settings, Harris gives others reason to respect him.

Drury had a similar thought.

"When doing seminars or working shows, I try to pay special attention to youngsters and women," he said. "You never know when just a sentence or two — a moment of recognition — might have a lasting impact on someone in the audience."

In other words, Harris and Drury conduct themselves in fashions that project positive images. Every ethical hunter should do the same.

In fact, Harris offered an anecdote about how a thoughtless slob once left the wrong sort of lasting image.

"There's a motel I used regularly through the years as turkey hunting headquarters," he said. "One year while we were there, another group of hunters cleaned their turkeys in the motel room, leaving feathers and blood all over the place. The management still talks about that experience, and the lesson to be learned is that one shameful action has left a lasting bad taste. I just hope some of my actions through the years have sent the opposite message."

Ethics remains an elusive concept. Yet deep down, every hunter has gut feelings about what's right and wrong. Be true to yourself, keep the hunter's faith, and let safety and ethics be a part of the mental gear that accompanies you on every hunt.

Gordy Krahn

On the Road

Thanks to various circumstances, today's turkey enthusiast is often a traveling man.

The proliferation of commercial airlines has made it far simpler to reach remote places, and the interstate system lets hunters visit nearby states with only a day or two of driving. However, ease of travel doesn't really explain the tremendous upsurge in traveling turkey hunters. Instead, soaring turkey populations have been primarily responsible. Increasing numbers of birds tempt hunters to sample greener pastures. Plus, add the undoubted appeal of various slams, the promotion of different subspecies through magazine articles and record-keeping of the National Wild Turkey Federation, and you realize the allure of venturing to new areas.

The simple call to adventure, a desire to visit new locales and deal with different subspecies, unquestionably figures in the travels of average hunters. The poet of the Yukon, Robert Service, could just as well have had turkey hunters as Arctic gold prospectors in mind when he wrote:

There's a race of men that don't fit in,
A race that can't stand still;
So they break the hearts of kith and kin,
And they roam the world at will.
They range the field and they rove the flood,
And they climb the mountain's crest;
Theirs is the curse of the gypsy blood,
And they don't know how to rest.

Turkey hunters seek their equivalent of gold, and anyone who has been haunted by memories of hunts gone awry understands the words about knowing "how to rest."

"There are all sorts of joys awaiting traveling turkey hunters," Drury said. "You see new places and meet new people. For my tastes, at least, one of the things that adds to the experience is camaraderie. Whether your companion is a longtime hunting buddy or a new-found friend, the togetherness adds to the experience."

For many, hunting new areas involves a subspecies different from their local birds. Four turkey subspecies inhabit the United States: Osceola, Eastern, Merriam's and Rio Grande. Every state but Alaska has huntable populations and an open season. In addition to the U.S. subspecies, Mexico offers a fifth, the Gould's. The remote jungles of Central America are home to another, the Ocellated. Taking the four U.S. subspecies, in one season or a career, produces a grand slam. Incidentally, Harris and Drury have collected multiple grand slams. A royal slam includes the Gould's, and a world slam incorporates all six.

No one has created another slam, but you can take matters one step further. The distant, lovely North and South islands of New Zealand hold a plentiful population of feral turkeys, the origin and nature of which remain in dispute. They closely resemble Merriam's in appearance, sound and behavior, although thanks to minimal hunting pressure and the absence of mammalian predators other than man, they are far easier to hunt.

Many hunters consider the challenges of slams appealing, and spring finds them abandoning hearth and home season after season. Of course, you can also pursue slams during fall, although to my knowledge, no one has killed a grand slam in one autumn. For an average hunter of limited means and free time, accomplishing any slam in a year, spring or fall, is likely out of the question. However, with some of what my grandfather described as "dreaming and scheming," a lifetime grand slam — or even several — are within reach. You can hunt public land or hook up with a local by exchanging hunts, or camp out and drive rather than flying — in general, do things on a budget.

Whether you pinch pennies or do everything first class, remember several considerations. Many come into play long before you hit the road, and the Boy Scouts' motto, "Be prepared," has great relevance.

You don't have to travel to be a first-rate turkey hunter or savor the sport's rewards. In fact, some old-timers I know have never hunted more than 40 or 50 miles from home, yet they're superb hunters. If you want to

THE OUTLAND EXPERTS have traveled extensively to hunt turkeys. Videography and the desire to film several hunts each spring looms large in their wanderings.

roam, however, seeking new horizons and subspecies, and sampling different geography and varied hunting techniques, can have real appeal.

The Outland experts have traveled extensively to hunt turkeys. Videography and the desire to film several hunts each spring looms large in their wanderings. Still, Drury and Harris acknowledge work is only part of it. They love visiting new places, and travel extends their seasons. As March arrives, Drury and Harris sing their version of the Ricky Nelson classic, "I'm a Traveling Man," and it's usually late May before they return home for an extended period.

Here, they share collective experiences from years of travel. Hopefully, they will help you avoid the road's possible pitfalls and instead savor such adventures.

BACKGROUND PREPARATION

Long-distance turkey trips, which could be defined as any excursion involving an overnight stay, shouldn't be spur-of-the-moment. Success and enjoyment require considerable preparation. Some aspects are obvi-

179

ous — getting the best airline rates, making lodging arrangements, and checking on meals and similar matters. Comfort and cost are always worth consideration.

If you plan to hunt with an outfitter, several simple steps can save heartache. Unfortunately, the outfitting world holds some fly-by-night scoundrels along with plenty of reputable, hard-working, operations. Make certain you book with one of the latter.

Ask basic questions before you pay high dollars for a hunt. What is the outfitter's success rate the past three years? How long has the outfitter been in business? A long tenure usually indicates solid professionalism, though you shouldn't automatically dismiss a relative newcomer. Are hunts fully guided? How many people do they book per hunt, and how much huntable land do they have? Large groups or small territories per hunter are warning signals. Do they charge extra for a second bird? Can they arrange for local taxidermy services? The answers will reveal much. Also, ask for several references, and call them. A few dollars on telephone calls can be worthwhile.

After your questions have been answered satisfactorily and you have booked a trip, let your outfitter know about any special needs. Many outfitters will supply a list of what to bring and a form that lets you define special needs. Incidentally, this is a hallmark of a sound operation. If you have special dietary desires, let the outfitter know. The same holds true for allergies, or if you don't — or do — want to share a room with a smoker. It isn't fair to wait until arrival to make demands that require advance notice.

If you plan to hunt public land or on your own, obtain topographical maps of the area, and study them in advance. Even when hunting with an outfitter, these maps can help you learn the lay of the land. Again, a few dollars to acquire U.S. Geological Survey maps will be worth it.

Unless you're hunting with an outfitter, try to obtain local information about hunting conditions. The local conservation office can be a good starting point, but making contact with a hunter is better. Often, you can do this on the Internet or at the National Wild Turkey Federation's national convention. Offering to exchange hunts can be appealing and might lead to new friendships and new hunting frontiers.

Finally, do some reading. Most states have wildlife magazines, and articles about turkey hunting typically appear seasonally. Outdoor maga-

IF YOU PLAN to hunt with an outfitter, several simple steps can save heartache. Unfortunately, the outfitting world holds some fly-by-night scoundrels along with plenty of reputable, hard-working, operations. Make certain you book with one of the latter.

zines, notably *Turkey & Turkey Hunting* and *Turkey Call*, have articles and ads that can help you find new hunting challenges or a specific region. In some cases, books focus on turkey hunting in a state or region. Finally, don't overlook free literature. State and local tourism officials will send you plenty of brochures and general information if you ask, and a state wildlife agency might have publications other than regulations.

Through study, some calls and attention to other details, you can lay the groundwork for your hunt. In fact, getting ready should be part of the fun. It builds anticipation, and there's a sense of self-satisfaction in knowing you have done your pre-hunt homework efficiently and thoroughly.

After your long-range preparation is finished, considerable work and planning remain. A reality of modern air travel is delays. This might involve missed connections, late or canceled flights and other inconve-

FROM LEFT, Tad Brown, Mark Scroggins, Jason Morrow and Mark Drury showcase the results of a successful 1995 hunt.

niences. Spring weather tends to be unsettled, and this increases the likelihood of delays.

"Whenever possible, try to avoid evening flights," Drury said. "When there are problems, they tend to worsen as the day wears on, and you are also more likely to have storms in late afternoon and evening. By traveling early, you at least have some time to arrange another flight or make alternative arrangements when something goes wrong. But encountering difficulties on an evening flight almost guarantees an overnight stay somewhere you don't want to be."

Harris usually hosts several writers and corporate clients each spring, and he believes it's helpful to have a list of phone numbers and flight numbers.

"If you get delayed somewhere or miss a flight, at least you can call ahead and let someone know about the problems," he said.

It's always wise to allow a little extra time, whether flying or driving. Checking in guns at airports invariably takes longer, and you'll occasionally meet someone who doesn't like hunting or has anti-gun sentiments. Be polite and patient, know the rules, and be sure you observe them. You'll likely discover some inconsistency and uncertainty among check-in counter personnel in knowing how they should handle guns, but remember a couple of basic rules. Be ready to demonstrate that the weapon is unloaded, and pack it with the breech open. Also, remember that you cannot pack ammunition with your guns. Put your shotshells in your suitcase or duffel bag, because ammo cannot be a part of your carry-on luggage.

There's also the problem of lost luggage. It's wise to pack a change of clothing in your carry-on bag for such eventualities, although this won't mean you're ready to hunt. If your luggage doesn't arrive with your flight, be polite but insistent in letting airline personnel know your problem. If necessary, as was the case during one hunt I took with Drury, ask to speak to a supervisor.

Problems posed by weather, airlines or other situations are, to some degree, out of your control, and they're the largest sources of frustration to traveling turkey hunters. However, you must also remember several other matters. Most involve equipment and planning. A checklist of critical concerns, whether written or in mental notes, helps. Drury and Harris rely on such "get-ready" lists and review them before every trip.

Here are some things to remember as you form your list.

➤ Weather. You must know something about the climate and conditions you might encounter. A trip to southern Texas, for example, requires snake boots or chaps and includes the potential for hot weather. In the upper Midwest or New England, you might encounter snow or freezing temperatures, especially early in the season. Florida — and the Deep South in general — can involve hordes of mosquitoes and temperatures in the 80s.

Always pack raingear, no matter your destination. Also, you'll want footwear that will stay dry even in the soggiest conditions. Drury pays close attention to the weather, and despite all the jokes about the unreliability of forecasts, he believes meteorological technology can help hunters.

"The Weather Channel and the Internet can give you a heads-up on likely storms or fronts," he said. "By checking www.weather.com and typing in the zip code for the area where you're going, you get a seven-day forecast."

Notably, Drury and Harris mentioned wind.

"There's nothing much more difficult than trying to call turkeys when you have strong, sustained winds," Harris said.

Drury agreed

"Without doubt, wind is your biggest weather nemesis," he said.

➤ Licenses and tags. After you arrive at your destination, you want to hunt turkeys, not spend valuable time seeking a license. Most states have arrangements that let you, with a processing charge of a few dollars, call a toll-free number and charge your license to your credit card. You can obtain this information by calling state wildlife agencies. When you call, request that a copy of the hunting regulations be mailed to you. Several states have limited access for nonresident hunters, which involves drawings or lotteries, and some have special public-land hunts in which limited numbers of access permits are issued. Usually, the deadline for these come months before the season, which is another reason to plan in advance. Depending on your age, you might also have to provide proof of passing a hunter-safety course.

➤ Hunting equipment. If possible, take two guns. You can find many good gun cases that handle two shotguns. That way, if one gun malfunctions, you have a backup.

"Always check your gun after arrival, because a gun case can provide a tempting target, and it's obvious what it holds," Harris said. "Also, you want to shoot it before hunting, and this is especially important for anyone who uses a scope."

It's best to carry ammunition with you. Even if you prefer a common brand and type of shotshell, you don't know whether it will be available at your destination. It's best to tuck a box of 10 shells in your luggage. If you place them in your vest, you won't have to scramble to find them after you arrive.

➤ Hunting accessories. As the comment on shotshells suggests, a vest might provide the easiest way to organize the accessories you need. A turkey vest is essential equipment, and it serves as a storage depot for an array of accessories, including calls; binoculars; a flashlight; knife; rangefinder; pruning shears; locator calls; insect repellent; first-aid kit; decoys and stakes; spare headnets and gloves; a hunter-orange bag or another turkey-toter; and chalk, sandpaper or scratch pads for slates.

Most of these items will likely stay in your vest, but Drury emphasizes double-checking them before you leave.

"I recommend paying particular attention to your calls," he said. "Make sure you have plenty of them and that they're in good working order."

If you have cherished, fragile calls, such as a box or wingbone, you might want to place them in your carry-on luggage rather than checked baggage. Airline baggage handlers have earned their reputation for rough treatment of luggage.

➤ Clothing and footwear.

"I'd much rather have too much clothing than be miserable," Harris said. "You can deal with a heavy duffel bag a lot easier than you can with adverse weather when you are unprepared."

You'll at least want a jacket, a change of camouflage clothing, and casual attire for traveling or wearing in camp. Pack extra socks and underwear, and don't forget your favorite hunting hat. If there's a chance of chilly weather, insulated underwear or a polar-fleece pullover might be wise.

Drury also suggested packing an extra pair of boots and plenty of socks.

"Comfort while hunting starts with your feet," he said. "No one wants to ruin a hunt with blistered feet or by having to wear wet boots."

"COMFORT WHILE HUNTING starts with your feet," Mark Drury said. "No one wants to ruin a hunt with blistered feet or by having to wear wet boots."

Also, Drury said breaking in new boots on a trip can be a mistake.

"Bring footwear you know fits, because there's always the possibility of a lot of hard walking," he said.

➤ Other items. Don't forget a camera, spare batteries and plenty of film. Today's point-and-shoot cameras work well and are simple to use. If you don't own one, inexpensive disposable cameras provide a satisfactory alternative. You'll want plenty of photos of your trip and companions. It's also nice to bring some special items as thank-you gifts for a local host or to recognize someone's generosity. These might include a warmly inscribed book or samples of a delicacy associated with your home area.

Alcohol and hunting don't mix, but for many, wine with dinner or a post-hunt evening drink add to the experience. If you have a favorite drink, you might carry it with you or check to see whether alcoholic beverages are available locally or supplied by an outfitter.

Don't forget personal items. Prescription medicines are an obvious priority. If you wear glasses or contacts, take spares. Make sure your shaving kit contains everything you require — deodorant, aftershave, razors and blades, and aspirin or other pain-relievers. You might also want to carry a book or two to read while traveling or before going to bed.

You should experience no trepidation about traveling in today's turkey hunting world.

"Travel lets you start early and work your way north with spring," Harris said.

Drury said travel lets him "experience spring not once but several times each year as I move from South to North."

You can enjoy multiple opening days, extend the season, experience encounters with fresh turkeys, and pick and choose the best hunting periods in various regions.

That's ample temptation to undertake turkey hunting pilgrimages and greet the glories of ever-returning spring.

Daniel E. Schmidt

The Crystal Ball
What Tomorrow Holds

An adage frequently used by historians says, "You can't know where you are going if you don't know where you've been."

Turkey hunters know where they've been, and no one wants to go there again. By the early 20th century, the wild turkey had vanished from vast portions of its original range. Many factors figured in this, including market hunting, habitat destruction, the absence of seasons and bag limits, and, later, the failure for decades to realize spring seasons made good management sense. Even three generations ago, the future of American turkeys looked bleak.

Henry Edwards Davis, who in 1949 wrote arguably the finest turkey hunting book, *The American Wild Turkey*, spent considerable time and effort trying to determine a way to reverse the turkey's sad decline. Others, including Archibald Rutledge and wildlife biologists in many states, did likewise. Generally, their approaches involved stocking pen-raised birds. All such efforts failed. Only when biologists began to use trap-and-transport techniques did turkeys begin their comeback.

Trap-and-transplant efforts started in the late 1940s in South Carolina. Before long, biologists realized they had hit on a promising method. In the 1950s and 1960s, biologists made appreciable strides toward restoration, and these gained emphasis with the emergence of the National Wild Turkey Federation as a conservation force in the 1970s.

Today, as we look back on a half-century of turkey transplantation and restoration, no one denies that the grand bird's comeback ranks as one of America's greatest wildlife success stories.

Men like Davis and Rutledge, not to mention call-making pioneers such as Tom Turpin and M.L. Lynch, would be astounded and delighted

189

IF THERE IS TO BE a future for hunting, we must pass it on down. We have many ways to ensure that our children and their families continue to walk a hunter's path. Pictured are Mark, left, and Terry Drury, right, with their father.

about today's turkey populations. They would also marvel at the emphasis on spring hunting, because fall and winter seasons were the sport's traditional approach. In fact, one indicator of how far we've come is that many states again have viable fall seasons, which provide a limited link to our roots.

Another dramatic change involves the turkey's ability to adapt and adjust to habitat. For decades, conventional wisdom held that turkeys needed at least 5,000 contiguous acres, mostly hardwoods, to survive. Thankfully, that's not true. Turkeys have shown they can thrive in agricultural areas, open country with scattered wood lots, suburbs with limited human populations, and even in the pine deserts that mark the mania of the modern timber industry. Not all habitat is equal, but given half a chance, turkeys will prove their ability to deal with changing circumstances.

The turkey would not have traveled so rapidly down its comeback road if not for sportsmen. Through individual efforts, membership in the NWTF and money from excise taxes prescribed by the Pittman-Robertson Act, hunters have done their part in sterling fashion. They have cooperated with state and federal agencies and private entities to provide millions of dollars and untold hours of work. It has been a labor of love.

However, hunters can't afford to rest on their laurels or bask in the glow of a sunny situation. Even as turkeys seem to thrive, farsighted folks are seriously questioning whether hunting can survive. For people who observe them, the danger signs are everywhere.

The hunting population is aging, and although recent nationwide license sale figures showed a heartening upturn — with more than 15 million permits being sold in 1999 — hunter numbers have decreased during the past decade.

In truth, an increasing human population is part of the problem. That results in an increasingly urban population and fewer folks grow up with a closeness and connection to the land.

Another critical social issue focuses on single-parent families, in which women are primarily responsible for rearing children. That means youngsters come of age without a sporting mentor. In days past, a father, uncle, grandfather or other male adult typically filled this role. Anyone who has read Robert Ruark's wonderful *The Old Man and the Boy* knows mentoring holds inexpressible joys. We need today's hunter-education programs, and they work wonders in many ways. However, a few hours spent mostly in a classroom that concludes with a simple test can never substitute for countless days afield under tutelage.

Also, we face the problem of rapidly vanishing public-hunting areas. When I was a youngster, posted signs were as scarce as hen's teeth — but so were turkeys. As big game — turkeys and deer — began to reappear, opportunities to hunt private land, at least without cost, began to disappear. This development — it continues apace with the per-acre cost for hunting leases increasing annually through much of the nation — was understandable. Wildlife suddenly had a dollar value, and landowners increasingly recognized that. We must hope that the United States, with its wonderful tradition of hunting access for all, never goes the way of Europe, where hunting almost exclusively belongs to the rich, privileged and well connected.

"Look at Texas, and you see America's hunting future," Drury said.

That is, he believes privatization, through leases or trespass fees, is what lies ahead. Texas has almost no public hunting. With the noteworthy exception of national forests, the same situation promises to become increasingly prevalent in other areas.

"We might not like it," Drury said. "but that's reality. The day of asking for and getting permission to hunt is rapidly fading."

Harris offered a similar outlook.

In my lifetime — and I'm not all that old — I have seen turkey hunting change from a situation where finding a place to hunt without paying anything was simple to one where a serious hunter is constantly seeking new leases or looking for clubs to join," he said. "We will never again see the circumstances our fathers and grandfathers enjoyed, where there was plenty of public hunting land, and elbow room wasn't really a problem."

An even darker cloud looms on the horizon. Arguably the No. 1 threat comes from an increasingly pervasive anti-hunting mentality. That perspective is most obvious with militant, meddlesome groups such as People for the Ethical Treatment of Animals, Defenders of Wildlife and other self-styled "humane" organizations. These private groups have talent for garnering media attention, and we face a bitter struggle to win the hearts and minds of the majority of the population, which is neither pro- nor anti-hunting.

Possibly a graver threat comes from the government. Without getting into detail, every hunter must realize that threats to our Second Amendment rights are reality. Look at the many lawsuits directed at gun manufacturers or the continuing efforts of the Clinton administration to restrict gun-ownership. For a bleaker picture, look north to Canada, across the Atlantic to England or to Australia. In these countries, private gun ownership has ceased or become extremely difficult. Admittedly, these countries did not have anything equating to our Second Amendment, but England has a long sporting heritage, and Canada and Australia are rich with wide-open spaces.

This brings us to the heart of the issue. What can we do to ensure the future of turkeys and opportunities to hunt? The answers are complex, but they unquestionably begin with something perceptive readers might notice in the "Acknowledgments." There, Harris, Drury and I pay tribute to our families. In our own ways, we thank loved ones who have taught us, tolerated us and walked with us through a hunter's wonderful world.

Brad Harris

AS BIG GAME — turkeys and deer — began to reappear, opportunities to hunt private land, at least without cost, began to disappear.

We also recognize that we are recipients of a proud legacy passed down by our parents and grandparents.

That sense of family closeness, along with appreciation of a rich hunting heritage, should convey a powerful message. If there is to be a future and generations to come are to enjoy the privileges we sometimes take for granted, we must pass it on down. We have many ways to ensure that our children and their families continue to walk a hunter's path.

Activism and active support of sound programs are the answers. We have voices, and we must make them heard. That can be done through voting, by supporting groups that lobby for hunters, and by letting local, state and federal elected officials know our views. For turkey hunters, membership in the NWTF is an obvious starting point, but don't overlook the good work done by the Wildlife Legislative Fund of America, the Izaak Walton League, the National Rifle Association and other sporting

Brad Harris

DON'T SUBSTITUTE one-on-one interaction with children. Brad Harris initiated his children to the turkey world early. Here, Brad Jr. and Jaimie hold one their dad's 1981 birds.

advocates.

We should support initiatives aimed at women and children. It's heartening to see programs such as Becoming an Outdoorswoman and Women in the Outdoors expanding rapidly, because that indicates hunting is becoming more inclusive. That isn't politically correct gobbledygook, either. It's reality, because we desperately need more women involved in turkey hunting and hunting in general.

The same holds true for youths. It's encouraging to see the NWTF's Juniors Acquiring Knowledge, Ethics and Sportsmanship, or JAKES, program thriving. The initiative provides a magazine for children and plenty of activities designed to attract and retain youthful interest in resources and hunting. The emergence of other youth-oriented magazines, such as one recently launched by Buckmasters and the Rocky Mountain Elk Foundation's well-established Wild Outdoor World, also provide interesting, informative opportunities for youngsters.

As important as these are, they don't substitute for one-on-one interaction with children. With mentoring, the "Take One, Make One" approach has great promise. However, don't depend on state- or nationally sponsored endeavors to introduce youths to hunting. Consider it a duty to spend some time afield as a mentor. Usually, you will discover that it isn't dull or tedious, but a privilege.

Drury mentioned another area for potential activism.

"Predators and their rapid increase concern me," he said. "We need to do much more work in controlling them."

Harris agreed.

"Turkeys have a lot of enemies, and maybe the worst of all are those that destroy nests," he said.

Skunks, raccoons, oppossums, snakes, foxes, coyotes and feral dogs can wreak havoc with eggs. If you own land, consider a predator-control program, or perhaps participate in the rapidly vanishing art of trapping. There might not be much money in today's fur market, but knowing that a trap line helps turkeys — along with the associated mental and physical stimulation — makes it worth considering.

The future isn't all gloom and doom. Turkey hunters should realize they have many things going for them, and should build on those positives.

"Turkey hunting is the best it has ever been," Harris said. "Right now, it looks like it will continue to improve."

Drury agreed.

"More folks are planting and managing for game than in the past," he said. "That's a real plus, because if you attract game and offer wildlife groceries, the animals usually fare well. Food plots have become a big deal, and without much question, they're an important wave of the future as far as game management is concerned."

Unquestionably, turkey hunting's good old days are now, and that has the potential to continue. Awareness, concern and willingness to sacrifice time and money for the resource can help us perpetuate the good times. How I wish my grandfather, whose tales seeing and hunting turkeys entranced me as a child, could somehow see how far we have come. Moreover, Harris, Drury and I hope future generations will be privileged to have similar experiences.

In the "Acknowledgments," while mentioning his grandson, Brayden, and the toddler's interest in hunting, Harris mused, "I wonder where that

Brad Harris

BRAD HARRIS' SON Brent at age 11 with his first tom, which was shot on Arkansas public land.

will lead?" We can join him in hoping tomorrow is filled with hunting and plenty of turkeys.

In pondering the future, let's again turn to the past. Rutledge was an accomplished, devoted turkey hunter, and one of America's most profound, prolific sporting scribes. He was also a sporting sage for every age, and some of his words still speak to us.

In his essay "Why I Taught My Boys to Be Hunters," Rutledge explained the philosophy behind his long, devoted efforts to share every available moment afield with his three sons.

"It is my fixed conviction that if a parent can give his children a passionate and wholesome devotion to the outdoors, the fact that he cannot leave each of them a fortune does not really matter so much," he wrote. "They will always enjoy life in its nobler aspects without money and without price. They will worship the Creator in his mighty works. And because they know and love the natural world, they will always feel at home in the wide, sweet habitations of the Ancient Mother."

Those words remind us that, as hunters, our challenge for the future is twofold. First, we must continue and expand our efforts on behalf of turkeys. If we do so, the great American game bird should continue to flourish. Second, like Rutledge, we have a sacred duty to impart our love of hunting in a deep, meaningful fashion so it endures unscathed and unsullied.

Acknowledgments

Everyone involved in this book owes lasting debts of gratitude to the partners and mentors who helped as we traveled along the wonderful path into the wilds and the turkey's world. Our collective acknowledgments are unusually long simply because our love for the sport is so strong. Each of us has, in distinctive yet similar ways, lost a corner of our soul to the turkey. Likewise, hunting America's grand game bird has significantly helped shape our careers. We are privileged, like fellow hunters, to live in a country where the common man can hunt, and where the turkey roams as freely as in the days of our ancestors.

JIM CASADA

No book reaches published fruition without input and assistance from others. As always, I am indebted to those I love. To my father, Commodore Casada, who first imbued me with a love of hunting, and who still delights in sharing tales of glorious days afield. To my late mother, Anna Lou Casada, whom I miss terribly. When I was a boy and a man, she encouraged my outdoor pursuits and delighted in cooking and eating nature's bounty. My wife, Ann, is a singularly tolerant soul, as wives of turkey hunters must be, patiently enduring one spring trip after another even as she assists in my work and performs miracles with the birds and other game I'm occasionally fortunate enough to take.

I must likewise express appreciation to the fine folks at Krause Publications. This is particularly true of Brian Lovett, with whom I have worked closely as a contributor to *Turkey & Turkey Hunting* since he began editing the magazine. It has been a pleasure to hunt with him, observe his evolution as a hunter, and see him become that cherished rarity — a writer's editor. His editorial skills have figured prominently in making this book, with which he has been closely involved from the outset. Similarly, thanks are due to others in Krause's Books Division, with whom I have previously collaborated.

Working with Mark Drury and Brad Harris has been a delight. My hunting skills have benefitted from their wisdom, and both are the sort of fellows with whom any hard hunter would be delighted to share a turkey camp. Finally, words will never suffice to express my appreciation to my turkey hunting mentor, Parker Whedon. One of the sport's genuine old masters, he guided my faltering first footsteps down an endlessly intriguing hunter's path and continues, years later, to be a constant source of inspiration and free-flowing fount of wisdom.

MARK DRURY

I can remember a time not too long ago when I would have been the guy reading this book rather than helping write it. Now here I sit, trying to acknowledge those who have helped me become the writer rather than the reader. There are so many.

First, I'm indebted to my wife, Tracy, and daughter, Taylor. Without their unending love and support, none of this would be possible. My selfishness in the timber has cost me many memories I would have otherwise shared with them. I'm blessed to call them my family, and I love them more than they'll ever know.

I will always be thankful for the great times and fond memories I've shared with my only brother, Terry. Not only is he my brother, but my business partner, guidance counselor, drinking buddy, legal counsel, banking authority, golf partner — not a very good one — but most important, he's my best friend. Thanks for always being there, brother.

I'm also indebted to all my family: Linda, John, Jared, Justin, Laura and Jason, Barb, Jim, Niki, Jodi and Waylon, Terry, Willa, Kim, Kelly and Matt, and Nancy, Gene, Joseph and Christine. I thank each of you for allowing me the time to do what I do. Without your acceptance of my lifestyle, I don't think I could continue.

Thank you so much.

I also deeply appreciate every person I've hunted or shared a camp with. Believe me, I respect you all deeply and appreciate all the thoughts and influence you've offered. To Tad Brown, Steve Stoltz, Don Shipp, Joe Shults, Steve Coon, Jared Lurk, John O'Dell, Dave Reisner, Mike Devine, Scottie Blair, Jerry Hale, Mike Mihalakis, Don and Kandi Kisky, and everyone else who's been there for me doing what we love most.

Thank you.

I'm especially appreciative to everyone at Outland Sports. Without them, my family and I would not be nearly as happy as we are today. Thanks so much to Dan Zarazan, Leo Tresniak, Louis Crider, Dave Billman, Terry Butler, Paul Meeks, Grady Fort, Jerry and Brad Valdois and, of course, Brad Harris.

One of the true blessings in this business is the opportunity to meet and hunt with various members of the outdoor press. During the past 10 years, I've hunted with so many writers that I am now proud to call my friends. To Jim Casada, Kathy Etling, Brian Lovett, Mike Hanback, Bryce Towsley, Jerry Robinson, Todd Smith, Lance Krueger, Roger Hook, Pat Durkin, Shirley Grenoble, John Wootters, John Phillips, Colin Moore, Bill Winke, Scott Bestul, Jay Langston, Nino Bosaz, Gerry Bethge, Eddie Lee Rider and Jim Spencer — thank you for your unending support. There is no power greater than the mighty pen, and you guys continue to prove that every year. Thank you.

Finally, I want to express the deepest thanks and gratitude to the people who started me in life. Mom and Dad, I love you so much. I can't express in writing how grateful I am for all of the love and support you have shown me. You guys have always been there for me.

Hopefully, I have in some way shown my gratitude by achieving the goals I have placed upon myself. Thank you from the bottom of my heart!

BRAD HARRIS

The opportunity to make a living at a sport that has been a tremendous love of mine since a young age has been a blessing, and I thank God for it. So many people have supported me through the years. First, my mom and dad, who not only instilled good values in me but always encouraged me to explore and enjoy the outdoors. When I had stories to tell, they would always listen. My brothers, Mike, Doc, T.G. and John, who made me work hard at perfecting my outdoor skills. My Grandpa Farmer, whose stories from hunting in the early 1900s fueled the fire that still burns so brightly today. My friends Dean and Dwayne Qualls, Charlie Zobrisky and Bruce O'Brien, who hunted with me in those early days when it was simply a passion to pursue game.

Many folks in the hunting industry have also played a huge role in my hunting career, including Bill Harper, who gave me the opportunity to work for Lohman Calls in 1980. Bill taught me much about the business side of things, and that took a young Ozark Mountain boy out to see the world.

Dave Billman, Jack Nelson, Jerry Valdois and Jock Lohmann supported me all those years at Lohman Game Calls. Lohman Pro Staff members Jody Hugill, Gary Williams, Randy Marcum, Billy Adams, Ronnie Robison and Punky Rose deserve thanks for their dedication through the growing years. Bill Jordan of Realtree camo has been a strong supporter and a good friend. Many outdoor writers have also been a source of solid reassurance that I am where God wants me to be. People such as Monte Burch, Mike Pearce, John Phillips, Jim Spencer, Laurie Lee Dovey — and, of course, Jim Casada. Without his dedication, there would be no need to write these words. Thank you, Jim.

The biggest thanks must go to my wife, Teri, and my children, Brad Jr., Jaime, Brent and Julie, along with my grandson, Brayden. Teri came from a family of nonhunters for the most part, but she always had an open mind and a heart as big as all outdoors. She has been my biggest supporter and has stuck with me through thick and thin for 25 years. If there were a Medal of Honor for hunters' wives, she would have a truckload. I can never repay her for what she has done for me, and words cannot describe how much I love and appreciate her.

My children would also have several medals of their own. Through the years, they have always been there for me and have gained a good under-standing of what hunting and conservation are about. My most memorable times in the outdoors have undoubtedly been with them. I am proud to be their father. As for Brayden — well, at 2½, he identifies all major wildlife species, owns a Red Ryder BB gun and is curious about what Pa-Pa does in the outdoors.

I wonder where that will lead?

About the Author

Jim Casada of Rock Hill, S.C., is one of America's most widely published turkey hunting writers. A son of the North Carolina high country who cut his sporting teeth on small game, he has "lost a corner of his soul" to the wild turkey. The editor-at-large for *Turkey & Turkey Hunting* magazine, Casada is senior editor for *Sporting Classics,* a senior writer for *Guns & Gear* and holds masthead positions with several other publications. Casada has been writing about the outdoors for almost a quarter-century, and has been a full-time free-lancer since taking early retirement from his position as a university history professor in 1996. He is the author or editor of more than two dozen books, and has won more than 90 regional and national awards  for writing and photography. He is a past president of the Southeastern Outdoor Press Association and the Outdoor Writers Association of America.

EFFECTIVE TACTICS
FOR HUNTING BIG BUCKS

Aggressive Whitetail Hunting
by Greg Miller
Answers any hunter's questions on how to hunt trophy bucks in public forests and farmlands, as well as in exclusive hunting lands. It's the perfect approach for gun and bow hunters who don't have the time or finances to hunt exotic locales.
Softcover • 6 x 9 • 208 pages
80 b&w photos
AWH01 • $14.95

Proven Whitetail Tactics
by Greg Miller
Both entertaining and educational, this volume, from one of America's premier deer hunters, explains effective strategies for scouting, calling and stalking white-tailed deer in the close-to-home locales available to most hunters. Packed with tips and tactics that spell deer hunting success.
Softcover • 6 x 9 • 224 pages
100 b&w photos
AWH02 • $19.95

The Deer Hunters
Tactics, Lore, Legacy and Allure of American Deer Hunting
by Patrick Durkin, Editor
Liberally illustrated in dynamic full-color, this coffee-table treasure examines effective deer hunting strategies and the mystique surrounding the magnificent whitetail. Also provides a thought-provoking look at hunting ethics in the 1990s, and the common bonds shared by hunters, the whitetail and the land.
Hardcover • 8-1/2 x 11 • 208 pages
110 color photos
BOD • $29.95

SATISFACTION GUARANTEE
If for any reason you are not completely satisfied with your purchase, simply return it within 14 days and receive a full refund, less shipping.

Shipping and Handling:
$3.25 1st book; $2 ea. add'l. Call for UPS delivery rates.
Foreign orders $15 per shipment plus $5.95 per book.
Sales tax: CA 7.25%, VA 4.50%, IA 6.00%, PA 6.00%, TN 8.25%, WA 8.20%, WI 5.50%, IL 6.25%

Credit Card Customers Call Toll-free
800-258-0929 Dept. OTB9
M-F, 7 am - 8 pm • Sat, 8 am - 2 pm, CST
Krause Publications, 700 E. State Street • Iola, WI 54990-0001
www.krause.com
Dealers call M-F 8 am - 5 pm CT, 888-457-2873 ext. 880 for information and a FREE all-product catalog!

The Latest Tactics, The Newest Equipment And The Brightest Ideas Turkey Hunting Has To Offer!

Get 1 year (6 issues) now

for just $13.95!

Credit card customers call toll-free

800-258-0929 Offer ABA2V8

M-F 7am-8pm, Sat 8am-2pm, CT

Or send check or money order to:
Turkey and Turkey Hunting Magazine
Offer ABA2V8
700 E. State St., Iola, WI 54990-0001

For you convenience you may order on the web at
www.turkeyandturkeyhunting.com

DISCOVER SECRETS TO WHITETAIL BEHAVIOR

Whitetail Behavior Through the Seasons
by Charles J. Alsheimer
More than 160 striking action shots reveal a rarely seen side of North America's most impressive game animal. In-the-field observations will help you better understand all aspects of the whitetail deer, from breeding to bedding. Nature lovers and hunters will love this stunning book.
Hardcover • 9 x 11-1/2 • 208 pages
166 color photos
WHIT • $34.95

Bowhunters' Digest
4th Edition
Edited by Kevin Michalowski
Hit the woods armed with the latest tactical information designed to make you a better bowhunter. This fully updated edition will help you find active deer, choose a perfect stand location and put your broadhead right where it counts. You know nothing tops the thrill of setting your sight pin behind the shoulder of a monster buck. Now, some of America's hottest hunters share their tips to help you achieve the bowhunting success you've always dreamed of.
Softcover • 8-1/2 x 11
288 pages
300 b&w photos
BOW4 • $19.95

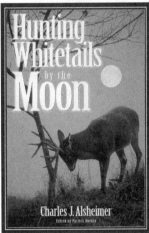

Whitetails by the Moon
by Charles J. Alsheimer, edited by Patrick Durkin
Charles J. Alsheimer, Deer & Deer Hunting magazineπs Northern field editor, explains how deer hunters can use autumn moon cycles to predict peak times in the North and South to hunt rutting white-tailed bucks. He details the ground-breaking research conducted that unlocked the mysteries of the moonπs influence on deer activity and behavior.
Softcover • 6 x 9 • 208 pages
100 b&w photos
LUNAR • $19.95

SATISFACTION GUARANTEE
If for any reason you are not completely satisfied with your purchase, simply return it within 14 days and receive a full refund, less shipping.

Shipping and Handling:
$3.25 1st book; $2 ea. add'l. Call for UPS delivery rates.
Foreign orders $15 per shipment plus $5.95 per book.
Sales tax: CA 7.25%, VA 4.50%, IA 6.00%, PA 6.00%, TN 8.25%, WA 8.20%, WI 5.50%, IL 6.25%

Credit Card Customers Call Toll-free
800-258-0929 Dept. OTB9
M-F, 7 am - 8 pm • Sat, 8 am - 2 pm, CST
Krause Publications, 700 E. State Street • Iola, WI 54990-0001
www.krause.com
Dealers call M-F 8 am - 5 pm CT, 888-457-2873 ext. 880 for information and a FREE all-product catalog!

Outdoor Books For Outdoor Fun!

The Complete Book Of Outdoor Survival
by J. Wayne Fears
With adventure comes risk, and outdoor enthusiasts need the know-how to survive in a dangerous situation. This book offers that information. More than 550 photos and illustrations support topics ranging from edible plants and animals to making solar stills and smoking meat. Each chapter contains exciting real life examples of people in survival situations. The revised edition of this highly successful classic is the perfect gift for everyone who loves the outdoors. Topics include first aid, survival kits, navigation, and signaling techniques. The most up-to-date information on everything you need to know to survive
Softcover • 8-1/2 x 11 • 368 pages
550 b&w photos
Item# OTSUR • $24.95

Spring Gobbler Fever
Your Complete Guide to Spring Turkey Hunting
by Michael Hanback
This anecdotal book illustrates specialized tactics and entertains readers with great ideas, diagrams and strategies for calling and taking all four subspecies of wild turkey.
Softcover • 6 x 9 • 256 pages
153 b&w photos/diagrams
Item# SGF • $15.95

Proven Whitetail Tactics
by Greg Miller
In Proven Whitetail Tactics, Greg Miller—one of North America's premier deer hunters—shares more of his insights and common-sense analysis that consistently brings down big bucks. This book picks up where his first book—Aggressive Whitetail Hunting leaves off. Miller's straightforward approach to deer hunting and deer behavior is based on more than 30 years of intense hunting and scouting on private farmlands, public hunting grounds and national forests from Minnesota and Wisconsin to Alabama and Texas. Whether you hunt pressured farmland deer or low-density wilderness herds, Miller has been there and can put you on track for success. This books generously illustrated with photos and diagrams that help explain proven tactics for scouting, calling and stillhunting whitetail.
Softcover • 6 x 9 • 224 pages • 100 b&w photos
Item# AWH02 • $19.95

The Complete Venison Cookbook
From Field to Table
by Jim & Ann Casada
Whip up delicious new recipes and complete menus for your next venison meal. Jim and Ann Casada cover the proper care of meat and field dressing, health benefits of eating venison and helpful hints for easy, inexpensive dining.
Comb-bound • 6 x 9 • 208 pages
Item# CVC • $12.95

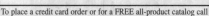

Shipping and Handling:
$3.25 1st book; $2 ea. add'l.
Non-US address $20.95 1st book, $5.95 each additional.
Sales tax: CA, IA, IL, PA, TN, VA, WA, WI residents please add appropriate sales tax.

To place a credit card order or for a FREE all-product catalog call

800-258-0929 [Offer OTB1]

M-F, 7 am - 8 pm • Sat, 8 am - 2 pm, CST

Krause Publications, Offer OTB1, P.O. Box 5009, Iola, WI 54945-5009

www.krausebooks.com

Satisfaction Guarantee:
If for any reason you are not completely satisfied with your purchase, simply return it within 14 days and receive a full refund, less shipping.